Advance Praise for
Generation Z's Guide to Work

"Wow! Where has this insightful book *been*? This truly is a treasure map to navigating life after college. The exercises act as an eye-opening way to create a-ha moments. One can quickly produce new results in their life by turning these meaningful breakthroughs into action. I'll be reading the various chapters again and again!"
-Suzanne Renee, author of *Conquering the Undertow*

"*Generation Z's Guide to Work* is a realistic approach that shows honest insight both into the systems of the workplace and the mindset of the generation. It encourages a sustainable method of implementation that will, given time, not only lead to work-place success but an overall higher quality of life."
-Emily Chauhan, Colby College Class of 2025

"Most resources that I've looked up regarding workplace issues are incredibly out of touch with modern day issues or offer Band-Aid solutions to serious problems. In contrast, *Generation Z's Guide to Work* gives valuable advice in terms of knowing my worth as a worker, self-care, and remote work among other things. All these helpful points are delivered in an organized and structured manner, which makes it very easy to take in. I recommend this book to anyone looking for a useful asset in improving their professional lives!"
-Francisco A., Generation Z

GENERATION Z'S
GUIDE TO WORK

What No One Ever Told You About How to
Achieve Success and Respect at Your Job

WINDING PATHWAY BOOKS

Nora Del Rosario

Jennifer P. Wisdom

Published by Winding Pathway Books

WINDING PATHWAY BOOKS

ISBN (print): 978-1-954374-05-8
ISBN (e-book): 978-1-954374-04-1
Book design by: Wendy C. Garfinkle
Cover design by Jada Fontanez
Photo credit: Diego G. Diaz

For more information or bulk orders, visit: www.leadwithwisdom.com

Printed in the United States of America

Contents

INTRODUCTION

As a member of Generation Z, were born probably between the mid-1990s and the late 2000s. Your generation is currently the youngest, after the Millennials (born 1980-1996), who followed Gen X (born 1965-1980), who followed the Baby Boomers (born 1945-1965), who followed the Silent Generation (born 1922-1945). Although many decry the whole notion of generations as arbitrary and divisive, there is some truth to the idea, especially for Gen Z.

There are three areas that set Gen Z apart from previous generations. First, you are the first generation to have grown up in a world dominated by smart phones and social media. Facebook and iPhones are not mere technology, but facts of life, like plumbing and agriculture. Second, Gen Z is on track to be the most educated generation on record. Third, you have witnessed a series of massive failures from global leaders. You saw governments brought to their knees by the 2008 financial collapse, the COVID-19 pandemic, and the looming climate crisis. In short, Gen Z has technology, knowledge, and a deep awareness of the world's problems.

With that awareness comes an appreciation for the ability of work to solve these problems. Many of Gen Z are more fiscally responsible and goal oriented than previous generations. Additionally, at the time of writing, the oldest members of Gen Z have begun to graduate university, and the youngest have started thinking about their careers. Whether you're a younger Gen Z or an older Gen Z, work is probably on your mind.

Like the world you grew up in, the world of work is in a period of massive change. As a result of the COVID-19 pandemic, the nature of work has rapidly shifted from in-person to online.

Moreover, young employees have started holding their employers accountable for social issues and their effects on the larger world. Much of the common wisdom and literature, however, has not caught up with these changes.

In addition to the growing complexity of the modern workplace, you still have to deal with everything else too: How do you deal with annoying colleagues? What do you do when your boss is unresponsive? How do you stay on top of a growing list of responsibilities? How do you get ahead in your career and make an impact? These are challenges you are likely to encounter.

Other creators are aware of this long list of problems and have designed a plethora of books and videos to solve them, but they're not perfect. Self-help and management books can be overly technical or hyperfocus on how a single person solved their problems. YouTube and TikTok videos prioritize being entertaining over containing a large amount of useful information. Even if you try searching for your problem on Google, your results will be flooded by clickbait articles containing only a sliver of actual advice. Where can you reliably go to for help?

That's where this book comes in.

You are holding a collection of nearly 100 work challenges. These range from day-to-day struggles to problems you have starting out a new job, to planning the future of your career. Some of these problems are fairly minor, such as managing email or learning how to talk to your coworkers. Others are more intense, such as dealing with bigotry or experiencing harassment. The challenges can come from your own bad habits, uncooperative colleagues, challenging bosses, or your company or industry as a whole. Regardless of your career, you are likely to face some of these problems.

For each challenge, there are 10 or more ideas for how to deal with them. The idea can be a simple action item, a general concept that can be applied in multiple scenarios, or a helpful mindset. You are not meant to try all the ideas out at once; check the "How to use this book" section for more details.

To help you find the challenge you are facing, the book is divided into 6 different parts.

Part 1 is Basic Work Skills. Think of these as the foundational skills to any job or just life in general. This includes how to stay organized, how to build relationships, how to interact professionally, and how to get help. Later parts will provide advice to specific situations, while these challenges can be applied to many different kinds of problems.

Part 2 is Career Challenges. This section is for you if you are questioning your long-term work plans or are trying to make the next step in your professional journey.

Part 3 is Self-Management Challenges. Here are the problems you can encounter when you sit down and are trying to get the work done. If you have trouble finishing tasks on time or are constantly distracted, this part will have what you're looking for.

Part 4 is Colleague Challenges. This section is full of challenges you may encounter when dealing with your fellow coworkers. These range from mundane issues like coworkers being too loud to serious topics like accusations and harassment.

Part 5 is Boss Challenges. Many of these problems are similar to ones you encounter with coworkers, but because of the power dynamics between you and your superior, you need to be more careful with your approach.

Part 6 is Company Challenges. These are problems that go beyond your team and your boss, problems that affect the company as a whole.

You may wonder, how was this list of challenges created? This collection used Dr. Wisdom's original *Millennials' Guide to Work* as a foundation to create something new for Gen Z. Each of the original challenges have been re-examined and rewritten to address the cultural differences between Millennials and Gen Z. There are also dozens of new challenges added which are either new to the 2021 workplace or are concerns more pressing to Gen Z in particular. The result is a combination of Dr. Wisdom's years of experience and conversations along with my knowledge and interactions of my fellow Gen Z.

Our hope is that your work will meet your lifestyle and career goals. However, when you're not sure what to do or where to go for help, this book is here for you.

Nora Del Rosario
Jennifer Wisdom
January 2022

HOW TO USE THIS BOOK

We do not recommend reading this book from cover to cover. A thousand pieces of advice are hard to implement all at once, let alone understand. Instead, we suggest you look through the contents, find your challenge, pick a solution, and try it out!

Don't feel like you need to try out every single idea. Each challenge includes 10 or more solutions. Pick one to try out. Stick with it for a week or so, and if it doesn't work, look back and try another solution. If your situation is especially complex, it might be worth trying multiple solutions at once. Ultimately, the real work is not in reading the book, but incorporating the ideas into your life. Treat these ideas as a starting off point to the ultimate solution that will work for you.

Throughout reading this book and in your work life, we say the best advice we can give is to be patient, be curious and to be mindful. Then show up to work.

Be patient. Remember that it can take a long time for a solution to work out. Just like how therapy or exercise can take months or years to get the results you want, same goes for improving your work life. This is where having goals and support systems can come in handy. They will remind you of where you are headed. Of course, if you feel like you aren't making any progress, it's valid to try something new, but sometimes the best thing is to keep at the grind.

Be curious. Be open to new experiences, new people, new perspectives. That is how you end up at your dream job or a supportive career network or your breakthrough idea. Most new ideas are a load of rubbish, but occasionally, you'll find something new, wonderful and exciting. The only way to find those diamonds are to sort through the trash.

Be mindful. Ask if what you or your company is doing actually accomplishes the stated goals and values. Keep in mind what you care about and what you want to accomplish. Your career is not a single problem with a single solution. Rather, it's about constantly asking "Does this work for me and for others?"

No matter how much advice you read, it's all useless until you actually show up to the job and get it done. You'll likely have your ups and downs over the many years of your career. Your understanding of yourself and the working world will develop and change. When you're not sure about what to do, this book will be here for you. After you read and when you're ready, it's time to get up and head to work.

Part 1. Basic Work Skills

Challenge 1: Determining Your Values

Values are more than just something for pretentious nerds to bicker about. Your values are your personal code. They act as a guide, helping you decide where you are deciding what career to go on or what kinds of friends you want. Because values are so personal, they differ wildly between each person. Thus, we're not going to tell you what to value. Instead, we'll help you figure out what your values are for yourself.

1. Make a list of the activities that you want to be doing (even if you're already doing them). If there are similarities, those might be a value.
2. Create a list of the people you admire. Often, we admire people because they embody some of our own values.
3. Think about your past life decisions. Choices like where you went to college or which friends you hanged out with might represent a value.
4. Consider your goals in life. For example, a goal like "have no student debt" represents the value of financial freedom or financial security.
5. Imagine yourself, 5, 10, or 20 years from now. Would you be happy to have the same friends or job that you have now? How does that reflect on your values?
6. Consider imaginary situations, such as a coworker asking you for help or your boss asking you to work overtime. How would you respond?
7. Look at the value statements of different companies, brands, or communities that you identify with. If you like them, you might like their stated values.
8. Take online personality quizzes. While they are not necessarily accurate, they can introduce you to language for describing your values.

9. Ask friends and family what they think of you and what values you demonstrate to them. If you don't like what you hear, you may need to rethink some things.
10. Ask trusted colleagues about their values and how they apply them to work and life.
11. It's okay if you don't know all your values right away. Often, the best way to learn is to go out and see what you're okay or not okay with.

See also:
Challenge 4: Setting Goals and Priorities
Challenge 6: How to Evaluate Yourself
Challenge 7: When and How to Obtain a Mentor
Challenge 9: When and How to Obtain a Therapist

Take Action: Make a list of 5 words that you really like. What kinds of values could you describe from those words?

Challenge 2: Setting Boundaries

Work should be an enriching part of your life, but sometimes it is overbearing or interferes with life outside of work. Boundaries are what you're okay and not okay with at your job. Setting boundaries is asserting those rules and the space you need with your coworkers and boss.

1. Determine your values. Having a solid idea of what matters to you can help determine what boundaries to set with your work.
2. How comfortable are you doing overtime work? Would you be okay working extra if it resulted in extra pay? What if you didn't get paid extra?
3. Would you have issue being given work that you think a coworker or your boss should be doing?
4. Are you okay with doing work outside of your job description?
5. What are your priorities outside of work? Friends? Family? Social life? Hobbies? How would you feel if you couldn't do those things after work is done?
6. Put your phone or email on "do not disturb" when you're done with work for the day. This will help prevent your work life from creeping outside.
7. Let your coworkers know that you will not be responsive to messages or emails once you're done for the day.
8. Practice saying "no" when coworkers push your boundaries. This can be in front of a mirror or with someone you trust.
9. Ask people close to you if they feel like your job has changed you for the worse. This could be a sign that your job is crossing some boundaries.
10. Talk to your boss about the expectations for work. Let them know if they cross your boundaries. While you

should have this conversation before taking the job, better late than never.

11. Acknowledge that some careers or industries expect you to devote your entire life to your job. Determine if you are okay with this long-term before moving further along this career path.

12. If setting boundaries within your job is too difficult, this could be a sign that this position is not right for you.

13. Work with a coach to establish boundaries between work and the rest of your life.

14. Ask your mentor how they handle work boundaries.

15. If you have trouble maintaining balance across multiple jobs, work with a therapist or coach to identify the common factors between those roles.

See also:
Challenge 1: Determining Your Values
Challenge 4: Setting Goals and Priorities
Challenge 9: When and How to Obtain a Therapist
Challenge 12: Working Through Differences

Take Action: What's one thing that you would not be okay doing at work under any circumstances?

Challenge 3: Networking

We hear about it all the time in job training or when talking work with friends: networking, networking, networking. Despite how often people praise network, rarely do people have good advice on how to do it. Networking comes down to meeting new people, identifying which of them you'd like to know better, and then building a relationship.

1. Remember that networking is about building long-lasting relationships. Don't just say hi or add people on LinkedIn; get to know each other and grow trust through activities.
2. After meeting new people, try to meet with them regularly over the next few months. If you offer one "hello" followed by a year of silence, they'll probably forget about you.
3. Give people a reason to network with you. This can be a shared interest (like sports or gardening) or a project they might be interested in.
4. Go over your current network and identify people you'd like to know better or who can connect you with new people
5. Get to know the people around you with a coffee date or planning a meeting over zoom. They probably would like to know you better as well.
6. Ask a colleague to work together on a project. Collaboration and asking for help are great ways to build trust.
7. Reach out to people you knew from former jobs or school. You'll be surprised how often they remember you.
8. Take on projects which will require you to work with new people.

9. Look for organizations based on your career interests. There are plenty of professional groups on Facebook, LinkedIn, Meetup, and similar apps.
10. Join groups based on your hobbies. You may get lucky and meet someone with similar career interests as you.
11. Attend conferences or in-person professional training. Face-to-face is one of the best ways to get to know people.
12. Identify people in your life who are good at networking and ask them for advice.
13. Talk to a mentor about potential networking opportunities.

See Also:
Challenge 10: Building Relationships with Colleagues
Challenge 15: When and How to Have Face-to-Face Conversations
Challenge 63: Colleagues are Overly/Insufficiently Social

Take Action: Message or email one person who you think would be interesting to talk to.

Challenge 4: Setting Goals and Priorities

Goals: everyone wants to have them and achieve them. But how do you decide what your goals are? How do you make progress on them? Everyone's goals will be different, so you have to determine what yours will be. Here are some tips to figure them out.

1. What do you want to have done by the time you are 30? Or by the time you're 50? Turn those desired accomplishments into long term goals.

2. What kind of life do you want to have in the future? Plan how you will reach that life and create goals around that plan.

3. Organize your goals into life goals and short-term goals (which should contribute to life goals). Shorter goals should be reachable with a few steps, whereas life goals can take several major steps to reach.

4. If you're unsure what to prioritize right now, focus on activities which advance your short-term goals or can lead to opportunities to achieve long term goals.

5. Consider if your current job is advancing you on your goals. If not, either change your role at work or find another job.

6. Make SMART goals: Specific, Measurable, Achievable, Relevant, and Time-Bound. If you want to learn more, there are many articles and guides available on the system.

7. Remember that creating your own joy can be a goal as well. Your happiness is valuable.

8. Remember that your goals don't just have to be career oriented. Starting a family or spending more time with friends can also be goals.

9. Regularly go over your list of goals. Update, add, or remove goals as you see fit. It's okay for your goals to change over time.

10. Talk with other people about their goals. They can give ideas for your own goals.
11. Consider how the goals of your workplace can align with your personal goals.
12. It's okay if you don't have a big life purpose or big life goal. Those come as you learn more about yourself and do new things.

See Also:
Challenge 1: Determining Your Values
Challenge 8: When and How to Obtain a Coach
Challenge 24: You Think It's Time to Move On
Challenge 42: Want to Improve Your Organization

Take Action: Get a white board or post it note that you see every day and write down one goal on it. Having it visible helps you to not forget it.

Challenge 5: Making Progress on Goals

In Challenge 4, we discussed setting your goals. This challenge is about how we achieve these goals. The answer: Figuring out what your goals are, determine what steps are required, and to check in regularly to ensure that you're on your way to completing them.

1. Make a list of your long- and short-term goals. This list does not have to be permanent and cover everything. Feel free to change it as you and your circumstances change.
2. Pick one or two goals to work on at a time. Focus on completing these first before moving on to something else.
3. Create a plan for accomplishing your goal. When would you like to complete it by? What steps are needed to complete it? Are you missing any required knowledge or resources?
4. Consider getting an accountability partner. Every month or week, your partner should check in your progress towards your goal. This could be a coworker, a friend, or someone you found in an online forum/community.
5. Look for someone who shares your goals. Compare your progress with them over time. See if you can learn something from their different approach. Be sure to provide help back!
6. If your goals are related to your current work, discuss with your boss about how you can incorporate your goals into your job. A good boss should be excited to assist a motivated and ambitious employee.
7. Think if anything in your life is getting in the way of your goals. This could include responsibilities at work or unsupportive people. Can you get rid of these obstacles?
8. Do monthly or quarterly reviews with yourself or an accountability partner to see how you are coming along.

What should you keep doing? What should you stop doing?

9. Plan with a mentor on how to accomplish your goals.
10. If you are having issues determining your goals or are unsure about them, work with a coach or therapist to figure them out.

See Also:
Challenge 27: Wanting Multiple Jobs or Side Hustles
Challenge 33: Hard to Finish Tasks
Challenge 38: Easily Distracted
Challenge 41: Want to Improve Your Time Management
Challenge 44: How to Build Good Habits

Take Action: Write down one task related to your top priority goal. Try to complete this task by the end of the week.

Challenge 6: How to Evaluate Yourself

In an ideal world, we would have a dozen coaches and mentors and friends always at the ready to give us feedback on how we're doing. Unfortunately, for many Gen Z, support like that is hard to come by. Fear not! There are techniques to give yourself the feedback that other people should be giving you.

1. Pick your short-term goal. Use this goal as the basis for your evaluation.
2. Get a notebook or a note taking app to keep track of your progress. Put the book or app in a location that is easy for you to access.
3. Set aside some time every day or week to go over your progress. This can be just 5 minutes! What matters is doing it regularly. Evaluations only work if you track your progress over time.
4. Keep your regular evaluations simple. It should only take a minute or two to see if you made progress on that day. Keeping it simple makes it more likely that you'll continue to evaluate your progress.
5. Develop a simple rating system for determining progress. This can be: What counts a great job? a good job? and a bad job? Use this to analyze your progress after some time has passed.
6. Don't change your approach too often. Wait for a couple week to see what happens. Approaches can take some time before working or even stop working after a few days.
7. Have annual or seasonal reflections to see how your life is going and whether you are making progress on your goals.
8. It's okay if you're not making progress. In that case, think about what is holding you back or what you can do differently.

9. Once you've reached your goal, reward yourself! Celebrate your accomplishment.
10. Remember that self-evaluation is no replacement for help from a professional coach or mentor.
11. If you are interested in daily evaluations, read *Triggers: Creating Behavior That Lasts–Becoming the Person You Want to Be* by Marshall Goldsmith (See the For Further Reading section).

See Also:
Challenge 1: Determining Your Values
Challenge 4: Setting Goals and Priorities
Challenge 14: Want Feedback
Challenge 43: Too Many Projects/Tasks

Take Action: Perform a life evaluation. Write down the following things: every major event or accomplishment from your life so far, what is your current situation and goals, and what you would like to accomplish before you retire. It's okay if you haven't done as much as you would like. Having it all written out will help you decide where to go next.

Challenge 7: When and How to Obtain a Mentor

Do you want advice with your field? Do you want someone who will help you make progress on your professional journey? Then you should consider getting a mentor. Mentorships are long-term supportive relationships with someone who is ahead of you in your desired career path. Generally, you will check in with your mentor regularly and ask for help when you need it. A mentorship will generally last for a while, whereas a coach will help you with one specific problem. Additionally, mentorships tend to focus on your career aspirations, whereas a therapist will focus on your life from a broader perspective.

1. Know what you want from a mentor. This could be general advice, career advice, long term support, or just a different perspective on your work.
2. See if your company provides any formal mentorship program or networking opportunities.
3. Go to local interest groups or online communities where you can find a mentor.
4. When approaching a potential mentor, talk about your professional background and ambitions. Let them know what you are about and what you want help with.
5. After meeting with your mentor, reflect on how you feel about their advice or support. A mentor should be helping you, not controlling you or giving you orders.
6. Don't push someone to continue mentoring you if they are no longer helping. Some mentorships last a lifetime, others only for a little while. The relationship can still have value regardless of the length.
7. Be helpful to your mentor when you can. Even though your mentor will be ahead of you in life or career, the relationship should also benefit them. You can

appropriately offer information that might be useful to them.

8. Treat your mentor with respect. Show up to meetings on time and prepared.

9. When your mentor gives advice, talk about how you implemented it next time you see them. This will let your mentor know that their advice is helpful.

10. Don't expect your mentor to help you out with everything. Ask them what they are comfortable giving advice on. Work together to figure out how they can help you.

11. If you think your mentor is not being helpful, think of what your problems are, what skills or experience your mentor has, and how they can help you.

12. Be kind and mentor others when given the chance.

See Also:
Challenge 8: When and How to Obtain a Coach
Challenge 9: When and How to Obtain a Therapist
Challenge 76: Boss Does Not Mentor
Challenge 93: Company Culture Is Not Supportive

Take Action: If you're not sure where to ask for a mentor, think about people in your life before who acted as a mentor to you. In what ways were they helpful? What did you wish they did differently?

Challenge 8: When and How to Obtain a Coach

A coach is an expert (usually paid) who helps you tackle specific problems. Unlike a boss or colleague, a coach is unlikely to have any conflict of interest in helping you. Coaches are usually action-oriented, giving you concrete steps to make progress on your problem. A coach is different from a mentor, who offers more general advice. A coach is also different from a therapist, who focuses on understanding, coping, and healing.

1. Look at American Psychological Association (apa.org), International Coaching Federation (icf.org) or other sites online for available coaches.
2. Determine what kind of coach you want. They can be a licensed psychologist, a field professional, or someone specialized in a specific skill like public speaking.
3. Ask your prospective coach about their style and strategies. How would a session with them look like? Use this to gauge if they are the right fit.
4. Determine what the price for the coach is. Some offer bundles with a discounted price for multiple sessions. Gauge their offering against how long you may need them for.
5. Consider if your company can reimburse payment for coaches. You can ask your boss or Human Resources for more information.
6. Do your best to have a clear and specific goal in finding a coach. For example, if you're worried about your career, you can ask your coach about making a long-term plan or whether you should find a new company.
7. Think about how you would like the session to go. Coaches often ask a lot of questions. If this doesn't work for you, you can ask instead for a more guided session.

8. Make sure your coach is not dismissive of your challenge. They should be supportive of your problems and emotions while trying to help you through them.
9. Discuss with your coach about what to do between sessions. Often, they will assign homework. These can get you to think about the assignment or practice strategies.
10. Pay attention to the feedback your coach will provide. For example, they may comment on if you are snippy, if you are late to the meeting, or if you reject feedback. This can be something for you to work on.
11. Be curious and open to learning!

See Also:
Challenge 7: When and How to Obtain a Mentor
Challenge 9: When and How to Obtain a Therapist
Challenge 16: How to Ask for Help

Take Action: Find people who have worked with coaches before and ask them about their experiences. Does working with a coach sound like a good fit for you?

Challenge 9: When and How to Obtain a Therapist

Sometimes, you have issues that run deeper than a coach or mentor can advise. Problems such as inability to manage emotions, severe anxiety, dysfunctional relationships, or inability to work, are more the domain of a therapist. A therapist helps you understand how past experiences can affect your current functioning, help you uncover bad behavior patterns, and figure out healthy coping mechanisms. Sessions will be more personal than with a coach or mentor and are focused on your entire life.

1. Determine what kind of therapist you want. Psychiatrists can prescribe medicine. Psychologists can conduct testing and give diagnoses. Social workers focus on family and relationships. There are also counselors focused on marriage and family. These professionals are licensed differently by state.

2. Get a referral for a therapist. This can be from friends, your physician, a university department, or a local clinic. Getting a therapist who is trusted by someone you trust can make it easier to work with them. Another option is to contact your health insurance about obtaining a therapist through a therapist network. Especially in the U.S., therapist networks ensure your therapist is covered by your health insurance plan.

3. Pick a therapist who specializes in your needs. Your needs can be specific problems like anxiety or depression. Your needs can also be someone who shares your race, ethnicity, gender, sexual orientation, or religion.

4. Look for a therapist who comes from a similar background to you. This can help you to build trust with them.

5. Remember that meeting a therapist for the first time doesn't mean you're committed to work them. If you don't connect, it's okay to look for another one.
6. Ask your therapist how long the sessions will go on for. Keep that length in mind while preparing.
7. Ask about cost. It may depend on your health insurance or the clinic or the practitioner.
8. A therapist should never undermine your challenges, your identity, or your goals. If they do, consider finding another one.
9. Remember that not all therapists can give medication. If you think medicine would be especially helpful, look for a psychiatrist or ask a primary care provider.
10. Remember that therapy is a lot of work. It is no miracle pill. Therapy is best if you have the desire to open, work, and heal.
11. As the sessions continue, have discussions with your therapist about your progress and whether therapy is helping.

See Also:
Challenge 7: When and How to Obtain a Mentor
Challenge 8: When and How to Obtain a Coach
Challenge 13: How to Have Difficult Conversations

Take Action: Talk with someone who has worked with a therapist before. Hear their experience to determine if it's right for you.

Challenge 10: Building Relationships with Colleagues

Relationships with your colleagues matter. Working with people you don't trust or don't even know can be miserable. Additionally, not knowing your colleagues can make it difficult to get help when you need it. There is a solution: spend time with your colleagues. Enter situations that build trust. It's just like any other relationship in life!

1. Pick someone you'd like to know. Send them an ice breaker email. Include a warm greeting and one reason you'd like to know them better.
2. Schedule a meeting to get to know a colleague. It's likely they want to know you better as well. The meeting can be over a coffee or a video call if you're working virtually.
3. Ask a colleague to collaborate on a task or project. This is a good way to know how you work together and possibly learn something new about the person.
4. If someone asks you for help, be prompt and do the work well. They will like you more if you are trustworthy.
5. See if your company hosts happy hours or other social opportunities. While still corporate, these events may provide a better social environment.
6. Try talking to people in the time before or after a meeting. You can walk with them out of the meeting room or send a message after the video call is over.
7. Identify what you want or need from a work relationship. Even in a job, relationships should meet your needs as well as the other person.
8. Practice active listening. Pay attention to what they are saying, then ask questions which demonstrate your understanding.

9. Speak positively about your colleagues during meetings and conversations. People will like you more if you're on their side.

10. Consider if your coworkers are not used to building relationships in your environment, be it virtual or in person. Offer them help adjusting. Share some ideas on socializing.

11. Be careful with sharing personal information. Oversharing may come back to bite you.

12. Do not gossip. If you have a problem with someone, speak to them directly. If the problem is serious, bring it up with a boss or Human Resources.

13. If you have trouble finding people you like, consider if your company or team does not attract people you like. If so, this position may not be for you.

14. Talk to a therapist or coach about your problems building relationships at work.

See Also:
Challenge 3: Networking
Challenge 11: Social Media at Work
Challenge 15: When and How to Have Face-to-Face
    Conversations
Challenge 53: Hard to Make Small Talk

Take Action: Say hello to someone you see regularly but don't talk to.

Challenge 11: Social Media at Work

While social media has become a regular part of everyday life for billions of people, we're still figuring out how social media should work while you're on the job. What social media you can use while in the office differs from company to company. Additionally, it is important to set boundaries between your professional and personal life online.

1. Know your company's policies about using social media at work. Your company may have strict rules against using it while on clock.

2. Determine what the company culture is around social media. Some companies are okay with you browsing if you get your work done. Some never want to see you on it.

3. Remember that your company will often track what sites you visit, even on incognito mode. Don't go to any websites that look bad.

4. Don't feel obligated to share your social media accounts with colleagues. Don't share what you don't have to.

5. Consider setting social media boundaries. For example, you can keep your LinkedIn to professional acquaintances and Snapchat to your friends outside of work.

6. Keep your sensitive profiles private so colleagues and bosses can't find you. This is an option on most major social media platforms.

7. If someone complains about you not sharing your profiles, be firm about your boundaries.

8. If someone wants to contact you outside of work, you can give them your phone or email instead of your social media account.

9. Be careful about how you talk about your company on LinkedIn or public forums. Many companies keep track

of what you post in public and may use that information to bar you from raises or promotions.

10.   Check if your company expects you to post about corporate events and promotions.

11.   You are not responsible for standing up for your company on social media. Leave that to your public relations department.

See Also:
Challenge 3: Networking
Challenge 15: When and How to Have Face-to-Face Conversations
Challenge 65: How Much Personal Information Do I Share with Colleagues?
Challenge 66: Gossipy Colleagues
Challenge 70: Colleagues Don't Respect Boundaries/Requests

Take Action: Read what your company's policy is regarding social media at work. If there is none, contact Human Resources.

Challenge 12: Working Through Differences

No matter how reasonable or considerate you can be, there will sometimes still be differences between coworkers. To handle this, make sure you understand what the problem is, then determine the best path forwards.

1. Make sure you understand the problem. Sometimes, the other person might be seeing a side of the problem that you were unaware of.
2. Be clear about boundaries. Having differing thoughts is no excuse to behave poorly. You shouldn't have to accept other people belittling your opinions or being rude.
3. Ask questions to make sure you're understanding the person's perspective.
4. Develop a solution that incorporates the best of both proposals. If there is no compromise possible, make sure the worries of both sides get addressed in some way.
5. Ask for advice from your boss or someone outside of the project. Getting perspective from a third party can help you see things you would not have.
6. If you feel like some voices aren't getting heard in this discussion, ask those people directly for their input. Just because other people ignore them doesn't mean you should too.
7. Don't make the situation personal. Keep the problem to the work and the outcomes.
8. Pay attention to the time and place. Sometimes it's better to listen first then ask questions later.
9. If the other party is not cooperative, tell your boss. Lack of cooperation is a problem that affects the whole team.

10. Determine who gets priority in your company culture. For example, sometimes the senior always gets final say. This will likely come into play when differences arise.
11. Speak to a company mentor about how they handle differences at your workplace or in their career.

See Also:
Challenge 2: Setting Boundaries
Challenge 9: When and How to Obtain a Therapist
Challenge 13: How to Have Difficult Conversations

Take Action: Write down the problem or talk about it with someone you trust.

Challenge 13: How to Have Difficult Conversations

No matter how good of a communicator or leader you become, there will always be differing opinions or misunderstandings. When those happen, sometimes the only way through is to have a hard conversation. Prepare what you need to say beforehand and be sure to treat the other person with respect.

1. Have the conversation as soon as possible. Better to address the problem now than let it fester and build up over time.
2. If someone does or says something that makes you feel off, write it down somewhere so you don't forget.
3. Outline your talking points beforehand. The conversation will be hard enough; make it easy to remember what you want to say.
4. Be sure to have a goal for the conversation. Sometimes you want an immediate solution. Other times you just want to share your perspective.
5. Before having the conversation, go over what you want to talk about with someone you trust. By saying your thoughts out loud, you will refine your ideas and be more composed when having the conversation proper.
6. Let the person know the general topic before having the conversation. Give them time to gather their own thoughts and feelings.
7. Consider setting aside a dedicated time for conversation. Some people prefer knowing exactly when a meeting is scheduled so they can prepare.
8. Make sure the other party has time to talk. A conversation is a two-way street.

9. Address the points brought up by the other person. It's one thing to listen, but to make the other person feel heard, you need to act.

10. If you can, avoid making the conversation about blame. Both sides should work together as needed.

11. Keep the discussion productive. The meeting should be useful to both parties involved.

12. If the situation makes you uncontrollably emotional, get support from friends or a therapist. It's okay if you have an emotional reason for having the conversation, but make sure you can handle them.

13. Focus more on the intent behind their words rather than the words themselves. This is especially important when working with people lacking in communication skills.

14. Ask questions to show that you care about the other person's thoughts and to confirm your own understanding.

15. Remember that no matter how much you prepare, this will be difficult. You can do this.

See Also:
Challenge 9: When and How to Obtain a Therapist
Challenge 15: When and How to Have Face-to-Face Conversations
Challenge 49: Overly Concerned about Other's Feelings
Challenge 61: Colleague are Difficult to Approach

Take Action: Set a due date for having the difficult conversation. Put it on your calendar or ask someone you trust to hold you accountable to the date. The due date can be tomorrow if you're ready or a couple weeks if you need some time to prepare.

Challenge 14: Want Feedback

It can be incredibly frustrating to receive poor comments on a project without being told what it is you could improve on. Additionally, it can be difficult to ask for feedback, especially when the person is harsh or insensitive. However, getting feedback is how you determine what is preventing you from furthering your career. Here are some ways to get feedback when it's not already given to you.

1. Ask for feedback right after the end of a project. The feedback will be better while the project is fresh on your colleagues' minds.
2. Ask your boss for feedback. It is their job to pay attention to how you are performing. Your boss may also provide possible areas of improvement.
3. Construct your own feedback. Make personal goals at the beginning of a project. Once it's completed, see how you measured up against them.
4. If your work is published or public facing, ask people outside the company for feedback.
5. Aim to get feedback regularly. If your boss or colleagues have a problem with you, it's better to hear it now than in performance review.
6. Remember to be gracious in accepting feedback. If you are hostile or ungrateful, people will be less likely to give you feedback in the future.
7. Consider your future goals when asking for feedback. For example, if your goal is management, ask for feedback on your leadership abilities.
8. Remember that while asking for feedback can be scary, it is important your personal and professional development.
9. Talk with a coach or mentor about your performance at work. They won't know as much as the people you work

with, but they can still provide valuable feedback from what they hear from you and their own experience.

See also:
Challenge 4: Setting Goals and Priorities
Challenge 6: How to Evaluate Yourself
Challenge 7: When and How to Obtain a Mentor
Challenge 10: Building Relationships with Colleagues
Challenge 76: Boss Does Not Mentor

Take Action: Before your next project or presentation, ask an audience member you trust to take notes.

Challenge 15: When and How to Have Face-to-Face Conversations

In the modern workplace, it can be easy to only interact with your coworkers over email or Slack messages. While these tools can accomplish most of your communication needs, some situations are best served by a face-to-face talk (either virtual or online).

1. How big is the conversation? Do you have a quick question, or do you need multiple paragraphs to explain your situation? The larger and more nuanced the issues, the more a face-to-face conversation will help.
2. Face-to-face conversations are good for brainstorming sessions or when you are unsure about what you are asking for exactly.
3. If you find yourself messaging someone back and forth for 10 or more minutes, consider switching it into a call or meeting.
4. If you are unable to spontaneously video call people or see them in person, consider making a scheduled event.
5. Don't bring in additional people into the conversation unless their input would be helpful or they specifically ask to be there.
6. Before approaching someone for a conversation, have a goal in mind. This can be asking a question or getting advice for your problem.
7. Ask yourself if you would be okay with the meeting going off topic. Some people like having lighthearted tangents. Others prefer getting straight to the meat of the conversation.
8. Ask your coworkers about how they would like to have face-to-face conversations. They may prefer meeting in person or prefer quick video calls.

9. Remember it takes time to figure out how to best interact with your coworkers. This is especially true in larger teams with many interpersonal dynamics.

10. Talk to your boss if you feel like your coworkers are using face-to-face conversations too much or too little.

11. If your coworkers aren't used to using video call technology, consider asking Human Resources or your IT department to host a training session.

12. Work with a coach to implement these steps and track your progress.

See Also:
Challenge 39: Can't Manage Emails/Slack/Teams
Challenge 61: Colleagues are Difficult to Approach
Challenge 62: Colleagues are Difficult to Contact
Challenge 80: Boss is Difficult to Contact

Take Action: Go over your past few text-based conversations (be it over email or instant messaging). Ask yourself if those conversations would have been better face-to-face.

Challenge 16: How to Ask for Help

No matter how smart or talented you are, there will come a time when you don't know what to do. And that's okay! All you have to do is ask for help. First, go over your problem. Then, pick someone to ask. Lastly, ask them politely for assistance.

1. Write down your problem or talk it over with a friend first. Being able to describe your problem can help you determine who to ask and what to say.
2. Pick someone that'll be a good fit. Your boss or mentor is good for general advice. Your coworkers will be better help for day-to-day tasks.
3. Practice asking. You can rehearse in your head, in front of a mirror, or with someone you trust.
4. Remember that the person you ask is often not obligated to help you. This can be true for coworkers or even your boss. If they don't help you, find someone else to ask.
5. Have a conversation. After they speak, let them know what you think about their help or comments.
6. Give the person as much information as they need to assist you. Don't make it harder than it needs to be.
7. Ask the person if they would like anything in return. This helps avoid incorrect assumptions about what the person expects.
8. Ask them if they would be okay to be asked for help again in the future. Some people are always glad to help. Others are okay only if it's occasional.
9. Be kind and gracious in receiving help. After all, it's you who's asking for help. (This only applies if they are also being nice to you.)
10. Regardless of the outcome, let the person know how useful their help was.

11. Understand that even if you prepare and ask politely, the person may not be able to solve your problem. It can be outside of their expertise or something only you can do.
12. Consider whether a helpful person would be willing to serve in an ongoing way as a mentor.
13. If you feel like nobody is available to help you at work often and you need that help, consider what kinds of changes would be helpful, such as seeking out mentors, finding mentors outside work, or looking to work for another company.

See Also:
Challenge 7: When and How to Obtain a Mentor
Challenge 10: Building Relationships with Colleagues
Challenge 61: Colleagues are Difficult to Approach

Take Action: Next time you need help, commit to asking. Write down a time on your notes or calendar when you will ask someone for it.

Part 2. Career Challenges

Challenge 17: How to Interview for a Job

Interviews are a dreaded part of the hiring process. But you are likely to have to deal with them if you want a job. Thankfully, there is a lot of information on preparing for an interview and interviewing. Remember that interviewing is a skill, regardless of your abilities to perform on the job. Just being a good employee doesn't mean you'll pass the interview.

1. Ask your interviewer beforehand what kind of interview it will be. It can be a behavioral interview, a get-to-know, or a technical one. The type of interview will determine what questions they will ask.

2. Brainstorm what questions they are likely to ask. Think about how you might answer these questions. If you have trouble thinking of any, there any many lists online of common interview questions.

3. Research the company. Learn about what they do, who their clients are, what sets the company apart, what the culture is. Having this information shows your interviewer that you are interested in the position, which they like to see.

4. Ask for interview advice from a mentor or someone you trust.

5. Practice answering interview questions with a friend, family, or even a coach. Rehearsing can make you less nervous on the day of.

6. Attend public speaking classes or attend an organization like Toastmasters International. These groups provide ample opportunity to practice speaking in front of strangers, while being supportive in case you slip up.

7. Make a list of everything you need before the interview. Your list may include your outfit, a notepad, and your research notes.

8. Show up early to your interview. Take the extra time to get acclimated to the space or get your equipment ready for a virtual interview.

9. Come up with questions for the interviewer. Examples include: How would you describe the culture? What's expected of employees here?

10. During the interview, keep the focus on the work. Salary and benefits can be discussed later, once an offer is on the table.

11. Write thank you messages after your interview. It will help set you apart from the crowd and make your interviewer remember you.

12. Even if you don't get the job, ask your interviewer for feedback on what you could improve on.

13. If your interviewer is moving forward with an offer, ask about salary and start date.

See Also:
Challenge 8: When and How to Obtain a Coach
Challenge 36: Feel Like an Imposter
Challenge 51: Difficulty Speaking in Public

Take Action: After the interview, write down what you did well and what you wish you had done differently. Refer to this list next time you have an interview.

Challenge 18: Starting a New Job

A new job can be an exciting chapter in the story of your life. That just makes it even more important that you start this new chapter off on the right foot. Here's how you can be prepared for your first few days.

1. Start a list of what your goals are with this job. Update the list as the months go on.
2. Come up with questions on important information, such as how to setup paycheck direct deposit, what are work hours, or what's dress code.
3. Make sure you have everything you need for the first day. This can include what you're going to wear or how you're going to get there.
4. If you need accommodations for a disability, reach out to Human Resources as soon as possible to request them.
5. If you're at an office, learn where you need to work. Some offices provide a traditionally assigned cubicle, and others allow you to work at any open desk in the office.
6. If you're virtual, determine what screen time is expected from you. Some companies track how long you're on your computer. Others are okay if you are online only occasionally.
7. Prepare for basic questions such as "What did you do before?" or "What you're looking for here?" If these questions make you nervous, practice your answers. You'll want to be authentic but also only tell what feel comfortable sharing. Don't worry about telling your whole life story -- people just want to get to know you!
8. Introduce yourself to people. Give them a quick summary: name, job title, department, boss' name.

9. Get the contact info of your boss, Human Resources, IT, and whoever else you may need if you encounter problems.

10. Schedule a meeting with your boss to get to know them and the company. Your boss is more likely than your peers to have a thorough perspective on the company.

11. Make sure to fill out all the required paperwork, including signing up for health insurance and retirement if available.

12. Find the people who interviewed you. Take advantage of the fact that you already know each other. Thank them for their interviewing. Ask them about the company and its employees.

See Also:
Challenge 4: Setting Goals and Priorities
Challenge 10: Building Relationships with Colleagues
Challenge 19: Understanding Hierarchy at Work
Challenge 90: New Boss

Take Action: Write down your expectations for this new job. What do you want out of the work? Your coworkers? Your environment?

Challenge 19: Understanding Hierarchy at Work

It can be frightening to enter the daunting world of corporate work and its corporate ladder. However, most companies follow a similar structure or hierarchy, with bosses on bosses and different offices to support employees.

1. You will have a boss, even if they are not called a 'boss'. This will be the person you report to with work progress, who is responsible to look over you, and will be your first contact with company matters.
2. There will be a chain of command which determines who has power and final say. Generally, instructions will flow from the top of the chain down, and those at the bottom report up.
3. Some companies will provide an "Organization Chart" outlining who has power in different areas. Even if it's not an official document, there may be an informal one available by asking around.
4. There may be an "open door" policy, where anyone on the chain of command can be spoken to regardless of status. Others may not. Check your company's policy before approaching someone far above your status.
5. There will likely be an Office of Corporate Compliance. Their job is to ensure that the company and its environment follow laws and standards. These laws can range from governmental regulations to rules the company decides for itself.
6. There will likely be a Human Resources department. They oversee staffing, professional development, employee compensation, worker health and safety, employee benefits, and labor relations.
7. You can go to Human Resources if you are being bullied or harassed, you need time away from work, you have questions about vacation, etc.

8. Remember that the primary goal of the Human Resources office is to ensure that the company is operating under employment and labor laws. They want to help you, but their primary obligation is to the company.

9. Larger companies may have a Diversity, Equity and Inclusion Office or an Equal Opportunity office. They ensure fairness and inclusion in line with government policies. (This generally means that decisions are based on employee merits and not race, color, religion, sex, age 40 or older, national origin, or disability).

10. If you have a problem, first contact your boss. They should know your situation best and may offer a quick solution that others may not have.

11. If your problem is your boss, consider going to Human Resources or to higher on the Chain of Command. Where you go depends on your specific company culture.

12. Assume nothing you say at work is confidential unless specifically told so. Your words may come back around to your boss or others, which may not serve you well.

13. If you're stuck with a problem, find someone you trust outside of the company, like a mentor, close friend, or therapist to consult with. They should care about you personally, whereas the company will support you insofar as it benefits the company.

See Also:
Challenge 16: How to Ask for Help
Challenge 11: Social Media at Work
Challenge 25: You Don't Want a Boss

Take Action: Ask around your company for an organization chart. If not, ask around to see who is in charge of what.

Challenge 20: Getting Beginner Work Experience

Most job postings have requirements such as "5 years of experience" or "expertise using this technology". But how do you get that experience or expertise? Sometimes getting a degree is all you need, but most of the time, you need to have work experience. Getting that first job can be challenging, so know where to look and make yourself as attractive to employers as possible.

1. Look for internships or entry level positions. There are usually many available on job sites like Indeed or LinkedIn. You can also directly peruse company websites to see if they have jobs or internships available.

2. Go to meetups, conventions, or online groups. Many companies like using these communities to advertise their job positions.

3. Ask professors with industry experience if they know anybody who is hiring. They may have connections to their former companies that can lead to you getting a job.

4. Build up soft skills, such as public speaking, writing, communication, and organization. They will help you on the job and help on the job hunt itself.

5. If you lack experience, consider working on small personal projects. These will not replace real world experience but having them on your resume is better than nothing.

6. Get certification or attend professional learning seminars. Such programs are designed around giving you knowledge that is useful on the job.

7. Talk to friends who have gotten internships. Ask how they got their positions. Their companies may even have additional positions open.

8. Practice your interviewing skills. They are common at low-level positions due to the low experience bar.

9.   If you get rejected, ask for feedback. Companies are usually looking for specific skills or experience and may reject you if you don't have them.

10.   Consult with a career coach on how to find beginner work experiences. If you are attending university, there is likely free career counseling available.

11.   Ask your mentor for advice or support in finding a job.

See Also:
Challenge 14: Want Feedback
Challenge 17: How to Interview for a Job
Challenge 18: Starting a New Job

Take Action: Set a goal for yourself to apply to (for example) at least 1 low-level position a week. You can increase this amount if you have more free time available.

Challenge 21: Choosing University Courses for Work

For many people, the point of university is to prepare you for working in a job related to your field of study. However, many times what you learn in school and what you need on the job are wildly different. Here are some pointers to help you find the courses that will help you once you've graduated.

1. Prioritize project-based courses. Regardless of your career or industry, you will likely have to work on projects or teams. Project-based courses simulate that environment.

2. If you are interested in research or academic work, look for courses that teach the theory and history behind your field.

3. Do some research on your own. Find out what technology or techniques people are using on the jobs you're interested in. Sign up for courses where you learn those techniques or technologies.

4. Reach out to alumni from your major. Ask them what courses helped on the job or that the alumni wish they had taken.

5. Consult career forums (such as Reddit) or industry articles to see what topics people in the field are focusing on.

6. Take courses that are specifically built around real-world examples.

7. Go to an industry conference. Take note of what topics are frequently discussed. See if your university offers any courses on those topics.

8. Consider applying for an internship. Those positions are often built with the expectation that you are still in university and learning.

9. Talk to career counselors in your university about what courses are popular or useful.

10. Remember that no matter how wisely you choose, university will not teach you everything you need for your job. There will always be things you can only learn once you get your feet in the water.

See Also:
Challenge 4: Setting Goals and Priorities
Challenge 20: Getting Beginner Work Experience
Challenge 22: Uncertainty Choosing a Career

Take Action: Look at what courses are required for graduating. See if required courses can help you on the job.

Challenge 22: Uncertainty Choosing a Career

Picking a career can be a daunting choice. Careers can last for up to 40 years or more. How do you know what work you'd even want to do for that long? It's hard to say for future you, but you can ask present you what you want and where do you want to be.

1. What are your needs right now? Money? Work experience? Freedom? Work/life balance? Look into positions and careers that fulfill those needs.

2. What is the one thing that would make you sad if you never did it again? This thing does not have to be career-related (it can be painting or playing video games), what matters is that your career allows you to pursue it.

3. What activities did you enjoy doing as a kid? Are there any jobs or careers related to those activities?

4. What are your interests? Could you imagine yourself working on those interests full time for pay, or would they be better as a hobby or side hustle?

5. If you know someone whose work sounds interesting to you, ask if you can shadow them for one day. See what the average day is like for them.

6. Think about what work environment you would like. Do you want to work from an office? Work from home? Travel a lot? Work in a lab? Visit teams on site?

7. Read the online article "How to Pick a Career (That Actually Fits You)" by Tim Urban (See For Further Reading section). Urban goes in depth on how career choosing fits into your life journey and what factors should affect your decision.

8. What impact do you want to leave in the world? Could your career be involved in that impact?

9. Where do you want to be in the future? Do you want to stay in the town you are now or move somewhere else?
10. Remember that your career is not set in stone. Many people change careers in their 20s, 30s, 40s, or even 50s!
11. Have a meeting with a career coach about choosing a career.
12. Talk to friends about your career apprehension. They might be able to give you some job recommendations based on how they know you.

See Also:
Challenge 1: Determining Your Values
Challenge 4: Setting Goals and Priorities
Challenge 26: How Do I Know If My Career or Work is Ethical?
Challenge 27: Wanting Multiple Jobs or Side Hustles
Challenge 28: Should I Work Remotely?

Take Action: Make a list of potential career choices. Add to that list as your ask yourself questions and talk to people. Once you have a long list, look over it for options that really strike your fancy.

Challenge 23: Company Choosing Uncertainty

While the job hunt can be a stressful time for many, sometimes you hit it out of the park and receive multiple offers from different companies. This is a good problem to have! But now, how do you decide which offer to accept? Figure out what you want and research to see which company is the best fit.

1. Determine your priorities and values for what you want in a company. Do you want to work somewhere you can grow your skills? Move up the corporate ladder? Earn a high salary? Do you want a specific company culture?

2. Research your prospective companies online. Websites such as Reddit or Glassdoor feature employee reviews and comments about their time working for companies. See if their reviews line up with what you want.

3. Reach out to people that work at your potential companies. Sites like LinkedIn will show you people in your network who work there. Ask them how they like it.

4. Send any questions you may have to your recruiter or the hiring manager in charge. If they have already sent you an offer, they should be happy to answer any of your questions.

5. Ask former bosses or mentors about the company. Does the company have any reputation in the field or industry?

6. Don't be afraid to ask for more time to decide. If they offer you the position, you can always reply, "When do you need an answer?" Good hiring managers should be accommodating to the needs of promising candidates.

7. Talk to your friends and family about the decision.

8. Think about where you want to be in a year or two. Do you imagine future-you being happy still working at this company?

9. Know your situation. If you don't need a job right away, you can choose to reject all your offers if none of them seem like a good fit.

10. Consult with a career coach on which company is right for you.

See Also:
Challenge 1: Determining Your Values
Challenge 4: Setting Goals and Priorities
Challenge 7: When and How to Obtain a Mentor

Take Action: Write down the pros and cons of each company. As you do more research and think about the decision, update that list.

Challenge 24: You Think It's Time to Move On

Not all jobs are meant to last forever. Leaving for a new position can be an exciting opportunity to grow and learn. However, as with any relationship, leaving a company can result in some feelings getting hurt. Do your best to leave on a good note, by respecting your team to the end.

1. Prepare a 1-2 sentence explanation that is authentic and diplomatic for why you're leaving. This will make conversations with coworkers and future interviewers a lot easier.

2. Give your boss or Human Resources department at least 2 weeks' written notice. This is a standard act of professional courtesy and gives your team some time to find a replacement.

3. Get the contact information of people you'd like to stay in touch with. Prioritize collaborators and mentors since they have the strongest connection to you.

4. Don't slack off during your final week. Decreasing your quality of work before leaving can leave a sour note to your team.

5. Determine what you need to finish before leaving your current job. This can be wrapping up a project or making sure someone else knows what you're in charge of.

6. Think about your goals for your new job or career. You don't want to leave your old job just to end up exactly where you were before.

7. Reach out to people after you've been gone for a few weeks. Maintain those relationships for when you may need each other again.

8. Instead of leaving your company entirely, consider switching teams/departments. Internal transfers can be easier than applying at a completely new company.
9. Update your online work profiles and resume with your experience. Be sure to include new experiences and knowledge you've gained on the job.
10. Make time for interviews, even if that means taking time off your current job. If you don't set aside time, it won't happen.

See Also:
Challenge 1: Determining Your Values
Challenge 4: Setting Goals and Priorities
Challenge 22: Uncertainty Choosing a Career
Challenge 31: Asking for a Raise

Take Action: Where do you imagine yourself in 25 years? What would you like to have accomplished by then? How will this move help you get there?

Challenge 25: You Don't Want a Boss

Do you not like taking orders or being told what to do? Have you had one too many bosses who had no idea what they are doing? Thankfully, there are many jobs out there today that don't require you to directly answer to anyone. All you must do is figure out which one is for you.

1. Determine why you don't want a boss. Do you not like being told what to do? Do you want more freedom? Having a specific "why" will help you figure out what you are looking for.

2. Recognize that most jobs require you to have a boss. Expect that you will have to put in more effort than the average person to earn a living without a boss.

3. Determine your situation. What skills do you have? What are your finances like? Are these enough to strike out on your own?

4. Research careers that don't require a boss. Examples include freelance work, starting your own company, or possibly working in a company with very loose management.

5. If your job takes a lot of time or energy, consider changing to a low-pressure job while trying to make your boss-free job a reality.

6. Consider if your current job can be altered to fit your boss-free desires. For example, if you want more freedom, ask your boss if you can work on your own time.

7. If you need to quit your current job, give at least the standard two weeks' notice. Be sure to not burn any bridges in case you need to come back.

8. Have good emotional support from friends or family. Striking it out on your own is not easy. You're going to need all the help you can get.

9.   Find people online who also are trying to strike out on their own for support and advice.
10. Attend local entrepreneur groups for ideas and community.
11. Consult with a career coach to determine your career path and how to get there.

See Also:
Challenge 5: Making Progress on Goals
Challenge 22: Uncertainty Choosing a Career
Challenge 30: Starting a Business
Challenge 42: Want to Improve Your Organization

Take Action: Find a role model who works without a boss. This can be someone you know or even an influencer who talks about how they became boss free. Use them as a guide.

Challenge 26: How Do I know if My Career or Work is Ethical?

You care about doing good work that helps people more than it hurts them. But how can you tell if you're company is one of the "good" ones? This is a question that many people must consider, and the answer may surprise you. Work through these questions, either by yourself or with others, and see what you can learn about your company.

1. Write down your career values. How do you want to work? What kind of impact do you want? What decisions are you willing to make to achieve that impact?
2. Ask yourself who benefits from your work. If it's a product, does it make your user's lives better?
3. How are people treated in your industry? Are people treated fairly or are they worked to death? is there especially high churn or burn out rates?
4. What influences decisions in your industry? Is making money more important than having positive impact?
5. Look into the environmental effects of your work. If you work in manufacturing, what is your carbon output? Where are your materials sourced? If it's a regular white-collar job, how much is spent on possible pollutants like flights or office waste?
6. Does completing work make your life and the lives of your colleagues better? Or do you have to put aside other parts of your life for your job? Would you be okay with that?
7. What is the trajectory of the industry? Even if your current work is unethical, does it look like these problems will be addressed in the future?
8. See what people are saying online about your career or field. Do they see some impact or decisions that you are

unaware of? What are the bigger conversations in your field about your company or its activities?

9. Talk to trusted friends or coworkers about this topic. What do they think?

10. Have a discussion with your mentor. They might be able to provide some additional insight with their additional experience.

11. Acknowledge that no career is going to be perfect. The question is what you are okay with.

See Also:
Challenge 1: Determining Your Values
Challenge 2: Setting Boundaries
Challenge 7: When and How to Obtain a Mentor
Challenge 22: Uncertainty Choosing a Career
Challenge 98: Company is Ignorant on Social Issues

Take Action: When working through these questions, keep them in a journal or single document. If you doubt your work in the future, look back on these thoughts.

Challenge 27: Wanting Multiple Jobs or Side Hustles

When your main job just isn't enough, sometimes what you want is to pick up another job or side hustle to fill in the void. Doing work outside of a full-time job is challenging. It requires good organizational skills. But there are many success stories, showing this path is doable and can be highly rewarding.

1. Determine the reason you want additional work. Are you bored? Do you want to expand your horizons? Do you want more money? Knowing your reason can help you determine what kind of additional work you want.

2. Remember that a second job can be taxing. If you are unsure if you can handle another job, consider alternatives to a side hustle. If you want to be busy, maybe join a club. If you want money, consider switching to a higher paying career.

3. Once you have a second job, know the direction you want to take. Do you want the side hustle to eventually become the main job? Do you want to continue juggling both? Or do you want to just try it out?

4. Make sure your side hustle has compatibility with your main job. For instance, it's hard to write a memoir if you need to be in meetings for 12 hours a day.

5. Acknowledge that many bosses and companies don't want you to have another priority. In that case, you may need to keep the second job under wraps.

6. Keep a calendar to manage your multiple responsibilities. Keep your important meetings for both jobs listed to avoid conflicts. Also, use the calendar to keep track of deadlines.

7. Make sure any supervisors are aware of when you are busy and when you are free. You don't want someone to

schedule a brainstorming session over a meeting in your other job.

8. If you want to start a side hustle, remember all you need is an idea and some time. You don't need to be hired by someone else to start working in your off hours.

9. Have a support system. This can be friends, family, or a community of fellow side hustlers. They will help you navigate the emotional highs and lows of juggling multiple jobs.

10. Find other people who have a similar lifestyle. This can be from a local entrepreneurial club or a forum like Reddit. They will be an invaluable source of advice and support.

11. Work with a coach to navigate this new lifestyle.

See Also:
Challenge 41: Want to Improve Time Management
Challenge 42: Want to Improve Your Organization
Challenge 45: Managing Multiple Responsibilities

Take Action: Think of a small project that you always wanted to do but never had the time. Work on it during your off hours and see how it goes.

Challenge 28: Should I Work Remotely?

The world has been moving towards online for many years. Some have even worked remote their entire lives. Instead of going to an office, they just log onto their computers and do their job online. Is this work and lifestyle right for you? Here are some of the unique benefits of remote work, along with the unique benefits of working in an office.

1. Remember that some industries and positions are more suited to remote work than others. Research online to see if people in your field already work remote.
2. Remote work is good for freedom. Without a boss over your shoulder or the pressure of an office, you can take breaks when you want and work how you want.
3. Remote work is good for travel. Since all you need is a laptop and internet, you can work from nearly any developed country in the world (with company permission).
4. Remote work gives you control over your work/life balance. Work is no longer tied to the office; you decide when it ends. This can be a good or a bad thing depending on your personality.
5. Remote work is good if you are independent and good at self-management. You must be good at working on your own, since your boss won't be around the corner to remind you.
6. Office work is good if you like order and routine. Many prefer the routine of clocking in, doing work, clocking out, then being done.
7. Office work is good for building professional relationships. Getting to know someone requires lots of casual encounters and conversations. Those are more

likely to occur when you are in the same physical space as your team.

8. Office work is good for environmental motivation. When you are surrounded by other people working, you are less likely to slack off.

9. Office work is good for collaboration. Instead of having to schedule a video call, you just have to walk over to your coworker to get what you need.

10. You might want to work with a career coach to determine what kind of work is right for you.

11. Acknowledge that sometimes you may not have the luxury of choosing. An emergency, such as a sick family member or a global pandemic, can force you to work remote.

See Also:
Challenge 1: Determining Your Values
Challenge 22: Uncertainty Choosing a Career
Challenge 40: Difficulty Working from Home
Challenge 41: Want to Improve Time Management

Take Action: Ask somebody who works remotely if you can shadow them for a day. See what their routine is like to determine if it's right for you.

Challenge 29: Going Back to School

While work experience is often the best teacher, there are positions or promotions you can only get with an undergraduate degree or higher. Going back to school is a major decision, so be sure it's the right choice for you and take advantage of the resources at your disposal.

1. Determine what your purpose is with going back to school. Do you want to further your current career? Do you want to explore a completely different one?

2. Consider alternatives to a formal education, such as obtaining certification or seminar training. Those are usually targeted towards people already in the workplace and take much less time to complete.

3. Check your financial situation. This is especially important if you need to take time off work to go to school.

4. See if your company offers sponsorships for going back to school. Often your company will pay for graduate school if you come back and use the degree for a promotion.

5. Consider if any of your current or past employment would be useful your school applications. Take advantage of your real-world experience in the application process.

6. If you want to keep working, research programs that can accommodate your schedule, financial needs, and interests. Some schools offer classes on weekends or after work hours.

7. Talk with your boss about taking some time off to go to school. If you want to hold on to your job, ask if that could work. If you are lucky, they may be able to hold onto your position until you complete your program.

8. Ask people from your past or present jobs if they have any connections to potential schools or can advise you on next steps.

9. Remember that going back to school is a serious commitment of money and time. Don't commit without thinking it through.

10. Talk with a mentor about the benefits of going back to school in your industry or career.

See Also:
Challenge 4: Setting Goals and Priorities
Challenge 21: Choosing University Courses for Work
Challenge 45: Managing Multiple Responsibilities

Take Action: Set a deadline for when you would like to make a final decision. Figure out what needs to happen between now and then, and then make it happen!

Challenge 30: Starting a Business

If you want to build a company or take charge of your own destiny, you may already be thinking about starting a business for yourself. Assuming you already have a good business idea, you need to manage how this new journey will fit into your existing corporate life and chart out how you will accomplish your business goals.

1. Determine your business goals. Is it a fun or interesting side hustle? Do you want this to eventually be your full-time job? If you're successful, how big do you want the business to grow? What do you want your business to provide or produce?
2. What are your current resources? What's your financial situation? How much time can you take off work if your business demands your full attention?
3. Consider how starting a business would interact with your current work situation. Do you need to quit your current job to start it? If not, do you have enough time and energy after your main job to focus on your business?
4. Acknowledge that starting a business is incredibly difficult. It requires lots of time, energy, and emotional investment. Do your best to prepare for the journey and plan as much as you can.
5. Look for feedback on how you are progressing your business, especially if you are new to entrepreneurship. Even if you think you know what you are doing, you might be missing something important.
6. If you must leave your current job, be sure to depart on good terms in case you need to go back or ask your coworkers for assistance.
7. Know that building a business is a skill. Even if you have a good idea or the industry expertise, your venture may fail simply because you don't know how to run a business.

Successful entrepreneurs often take many tries before something works.

8. Research if there are any local entrepreneur groups. These are especially popular in larger cities. They will usually host information sharing panels and are a good place to network with other small businesses or startups.

9. Find a mentor or coach who specializes in helping people start their own business.

10. Get a therapist to assist you when dealing with the highs and lows of managing a business.

See Also:
Challenge 7: When and How to Obtain a Mentor
Challenge 16: How to Ask for Help
Challenge 27: Wanting Multiple Jobs or Side Hustles
Challenge 32: You Want to Increase Your Influence

Take Action: Create a timeline for how you would like your business to develop. Even if it's wildly off, having some plan is better than nothing at all.

Challenge 31: Asking for a Raise

The dreaded "asking for a raise" conversation: Just thinking about this talk can induce immense anxiety. However, this talk is the only way to get the pay you deserve. If you've already proved your worth, asking for a raise is just about showing that worth to your boss.

1. Create a list of reasons for why you deserve a raise. This should be related to your work accomplishments, not "I need more money."

2. Mention what value you've brought the team and completed deliverables. Instead of saying "I worked really hard", say "I completed project X which helped us Y."

3. Practice the conversation beforehand. You can practice with a coach or trusted friend.

4. Research the salary figures for your position. If you're being paid under average, include this in your talking points.

5. Make sure your boss is aware of your contributions throughout the year and not just during raise season.

6. Learn how raises are delivered at this company. Sometimes raises are only offered at the start of the new year or after performance reviews.

7. Wait until you've worked in your position at least a year before asking for a raise (unless you complete something major). This gives time for your boss to know your work.

8. Consider framing a raise as an investment from your boss into your development and the future of the organization.

9. During the conversation, keep the discussion on your performance at work and added benefits to your company and team.

10. If your boss says no, ask them what you can do differently to receive a raise in the future.

11. Remember that, in some industries, you can only get a raise by moving to another company.

See Also:
Challenge 6: How to Evaluate Yourself
Challenge 7: When and How to Obtain a Mentor
Challenge 13: How to Have Difficult Conversations
Challenge 80: Boss is Difficult to Contact

Take Action: Even if you don't want a raise right now, create a list of reasons why you deserve one. As you continue working, update that list.

Challenge 32: You Want to Increase Your Influence

It can be incredibly fulfilling to develop great ideas. However, many people also want those great ideas to be heard. Having influence can help. The more influence you have, the more likely people are to listen to you. You can grow your influence by increasing people's awareness of you, both inside and outside of your company.

1. Do work and have ideas that matter to you. It's easier to gain influence when you are a strong believer in yourself.
2. Determine how influence will help you achieve your goals. For example, do you need influence to get your dream project started?
3. Develop mentor relationships with people who wield influence. While your work should be able to stand on its own, having some authority behind it can help.
4. Improve your public speaking. People who can speak clearly and confidently are often seen as more influential.
5. Look for speaking opportunities among your team, at your company, and at conferences. You can speak about the outcomes of your work or your experience working on a project. Get the word out there about yourself.
6. Take leadership roles at your company. Overseeing others is a way to spread your influence.
7. Speak to coworkers about your work contributions.
8. Attend company social events and talk to others about your work. There may be people at your company who are completely unaware of what you do.
9. Arrange meetings with company seniors about your work. Some may be delighted to hear what younger employees are up to.

10. Build your social media presence. This can be a good way to publicize your work or announce your presence at conferences.

11. Read books such as *Influence* by Robert Cialdini or *Influence Without Authority* by Allan Cohen and David Bradford (See the For Further Reading section).

12. Work with a coach to develop strategies to increase your influence.

See Also:
Challenge 8: When and How to Obtain a Coach
Challenge 10: Building Relationships with Colleagues
Challenge 11: Social Media at Work

Take Action: Keep a list of people who might be interested in new ideas or projects you have to share. See that list grow as you expand your influence.

Part 3. Self-Management Challenges

Challenge 33: Hard-to-Finish Tasks

Sometimes your work can feel unmanageable. Sometimes you spend hours working, but it feels like you're getting nothing done. Sometimes you say you're going to start a task then never finish it. These are common problems facing many young professionals as they enter the workforce. Thankfully, there are many time-honored techniques for managing your tasks and getting them done.

1. Keep a list of your tasks or projects. Make each entry small but meaningful. Checking an item off should feel like you got something done.

2. Designate one or two things each day as "must get done." Keeping a narrow focus is easier to manage and gives you a better sense of accomplishment.

3. Consider getting an app to manage your tasks. Popular choices include: ToDoist, Remember the Milk, Things 3. Remember the apps won't solve all your problems, but they can make organization easier.

4. Consider changing your work style. You may work better with longer focus sessions or work better in quick bursts.

5. Find places where you can work without distractions.

6. If you have a lot of meetings or don't know when to work, try time blocking. This is done by adding 1-2 hour events to your calendar dedicated to important tasks. Time blocking is good for tasks which require stretches of uninterrupted time, such as writing or coding.

7. For every task, determine how it important it is for you to complete it. You may realize that you can drop the task or that you're not the right person for the work.

8. Consider if you can delegate the task to someone who can complete it faster or better.

9. If you get interrupted or asked to work on something else, say "I'll get to this once I'm done with my current task."
10. If one task feels like it goes on forever, discuss with your boss about splitting up the work to give it to multiple people or extending your due date.
11. Talk with boss if you feel like you're getting too many tasks.
12. Read the book *Getting Things Done* by David Allen or summaries of it online (See the For Further Reading section). It's a classic, and much of its advice and strategies are still relevant.

See Also:
Challenge 9: When and How to Obtain a Therapist
Challenge 16: How to Ask for Help
Challenge 40: Difficulty Working from Home
Challenge 41: Want to Improve Your Time Management
Challenge 44: How to Build Good Habits

Take Action: Find an accountability partner who will keep you on track for managing your tasks. This can be a friend or a trusted coworker.

Challenge 34: Unmotivated at Work

Everyone has times when we feel down and not able to do much work. This can be a sign that you need a break, that you need to remotivate, or that you're changing as a person.

1. Ask for a task or project that's different from your usual work. Sometimes all you need is a change of pace.

2. If you can, take a few days off work. When you come back, you can return with a clear head and see your work from a new angle.

3. Find work that you can do without being at 100%. This can be responding to emails or taking care of paperwork. Accomplishing something small but meaningful can get you out of a rut.

4. Think about what used to excite you about your work. Ask yourself what changed since then and if you can find that excitement again.

5. Establish stronger boundaries between work and the rest of your life. It can be hard to stay motivated when work feels like your entire life.

6. Take up hobbies outside of work. Surprisingly, fun engagements outside of work can motivate you back in the office or offer a fresh perspective.

7. Remember why you took this job. If this job is part of a larger goal (like owning a house or a promotion), remember that goal when you're not motivated to work.

8. Consider whether life outside of work, like an annoying commute or a struggling relationship, could affect your performance and motivation at work. If so, address those challenges!

9. Ask your colleagues about what motivates them. You may find something new to motivate you or learn something interesting.

10. Consider that your life situation may have changed since you started this job, and it may no longer be for you.

See Also:
Challenge 4: Setting Goals and Priorities
Challenge 37: Feel Negative about Work
Challenge 99: Company is Boring

Take Action: Make a list of what gives you joy and energy. Then, pick one item from that list that you can incorporate into your work life or make more present in your life outside of work.

Challenge 35: Feel Isolated

Work usually takes up most of our waking hours. While this is fine for many, workdays can be exhausting and demoralizing if you feel isolated. The best solution to isolation? Build up relationships both inside and outside of the office!

1. Reach out to friends and family to catch up. You'll be surprised how often they'll be excited to hear from you.

2. Find local clubs, community centers, or online meetups that line up with your interests. This is a great way to meet other like-minded people.

3. Strengthen your current non-work relationships. Setup dates and hangouts to ensure you have quality time with the people that matter.

4. Use apps like Meetup or Facebook Groups or Eventbrite to find local events to meet people.

5. Arrange casual meetings for coffee or lunch with your coworkers, even if only online. Get to know them better. Even one or two of these can make your workplace feel much friendlier.

6. See if your company provides any social activities or mixers. If you like your company, you are bound to find someone you like at an event.

7. Let your boss know you're looking to expand your network. Ask them if there's anyone who they think you'd get along with. Your boss can act as a professional wingman.

8. If you feel like there is nobody at your job you would like to get to know better, consider that this company is no longer for you.

9. Go to conferences related to your field. There you'll be surrounded by tons of people. There will be others trying to meet people as well.

10. Work with a coach to develop strategies on meeting people and building relationships.

See Also:
Challenge 10: Building Relationships with Colleagues
Challenge 54: You Feel Like You're not Heard
Challenge 84: Don't Feel Supported by Boss
Challenge 92: Not Sure Where to Go for Help

Take Action: Plan one activity this month where you will spend time with someone or attempt to meet someone new.

Challenge 36: Feel Like an Imposter

You may be familiar with the concept of 'Imposter Syndrome', the nagging feeling that you're not good enough for this role or that your acceptance was a fluke. There is nothing wrong with doubting yourself as you go through life. Some people experience imposter syndrome on and off throughout their career. The good news is that there are ways to get through these feelings. Either remember why you are worthy in the first place or build skills to boost your confidence.

1. Remember that you got the job. Your hiring manager or boss believed that you were the right fit for the position.
2. Create a "life resume" that highlights important events and accomplishments. Look at this when you are feeling down. Even the act of making the resume can be empowering.
3. Look for work opportunities that you can do well in. A new project that fits your skills or a task where you can provide a fresh perspective can help you realize what you contribute.
4. Remember that at work, your main priority is to get your work done to your best ability. It's alright if you're not perfect or accomplish all the work possible.
5. Make a list of what skills and knowledge you can provide. Even if you aren't special or "the guy", there are still ways you can add value to a project.
6. Identify areas you feel lacking in. Research how you can improve in those areas.
7. Look for interesting opportunities. These can be projects where you can learn a lot or joining teams with people you would like to collaborate with.
8. Get formal certification or training in an area you'd like increase your skills. Some companies offer these for free.

9. Talk with someone like a trusted friend or mentor about these feelings.

10. Have a conversation with your boss to see if they think you are up to par. You can say, "I'm looking for feedback on how I'm doing and how I can improve."

See Also:
Challenge 6: How to Evaluate Yourself
Challenge 9: When and How to Obtain a Therapist
Challenge 18: Starting a New Job

Take Action: What are you most proud of having done in your life? Write this down where you can see it regularly as a reminder that you're great.

Challenge 37: Feel Negative about Work

It's okay to complain about work every once in a while. You may come to a point, however, where the thought of clocking in fills you with dread or anger or frustration. Persistent negative emotions can impact your health, your non-work relationships, and your ability to do your work. Unfortunately, this can be caused by any number of problems. Focus on figuring out the cause and weeding out the issue.

1. Look over your long- and short-term goals. Consider if your work is still progressing you towards them. Lacking a sense of progress can make you feel like you're stuck or not doing anything meaningful.
2. Update your resume with your recent accomplishments. Remind yourself of the great work you have done.
3. Determine what about your work is really bringing you down. Is it the company, your team, your boss? Is it the work itself?
4. Write down 5 good things about your job.
5. Emotions can be fleeting. You may find the negative feelings go away with time. Distraction can help!
6. Ask yourself if the negativity is tied to boredom. If so, you can ask for something different from your usual work.
7. Determine if you've worked too long without a break. Going for months without a vacation can lead to burnout.
8. Consider if your work environment is a contributing factor. Being surrounded by complainers and gossipers can bring down anyone's mood.
9. Think about your life outside of work. Problems at home can lead to negative feelings about the rest of your life, including work.
10. Ask if you feel like an imposter.

11. Write down a list of your negative thought patterns. Come up with responses to when they come up. A therapist can help with this.

12. Consider if you'd be happier working at a different company.

See Also:
Challenge 9: When and How to Obtain a Therapist
Challenge 24: You Think It's Time to Move On
Challenge 36: Feel Like an Imposter
Challenge 56: Meetings are Frustrating

Take Action: Remember that negative emotions are not your fault, but you are still responsible for taking care of them. What are the negative emotions you're experiencing, and what would you like to feel instead? What can you do to get to those better emotions?

Challenge 38: Easily Distracted

It can be incredibly frustrating to find yourself continually getting distracted from your work, especially if there's an important deadline looming ahead. Unfortunately, there are countless possible sources of distraction, from the noises of the office to the endless buzz of the internet. Here are a few ways to identify and deal with some of those distractions.

1. Imagine what your ideal working environment would be. Some people like to work in a bustling café; others prefer a silent study room.

2. Consider wearing headphones if your situation allows. This is an easy solution to noisy neighbors and loud background activities.

3. Put your phone on "Do not disturb" and mute your computer. The sudden bleeps of emails or texts can easily pull you out of the work zone.

4. Consider working at less busy times of day. There is likely to be less noisy activity early in the morning or later at night.

5. If you find yourself distracted by the internet, consider uninstalling the apps from your phone or installing website blockers on your computer browser.

6. Take a break. Go for a walk. Distractions can be easier to ignore after giving your mind a quick reset.

7. Add focus time events to your calendar. Make a small commitment to yourself to focus solely on your important tasks during this time.

8. Write down the one thing that must happen today. Having one goal per day can make it easier to focus.

9. Consider if the distractions are really a problem. If you are getting your work done well and on time, you may not need to make any changes.

10. Consider if you find your work boring. Ask your boss if there are more interesting tasks available. Possibly, this position may no longer be for you.
11. If distractibility is an issue for a long time or affects your life outside of work, you may want to seek medical advice. Talk with a doctor or a psychiatrist.
12. Talk with a coach to develop plans to deal with distractions.

See Also:
Challenge 33: Hard to Finish Tasks
Challenge 40: Difficulty Working from Home
Challenge 44: How to Build Good Habits
Challenge 57: Annoying Office Mate

Take Action: Identify one distraction that keeps appearing and make a plan to deal with it.

Challenge 39: Can't Manage Emails/Slack/Teams

The modern workplace is dominated by email, Slack, and Microsoft Teams. While convenient, these tools make it so easy for people to message you that you can end up getting swamped with a sea of messages. Having to sort out the useful messages from the nonsense can be frustrating. Just seeing a massive pile of emails or unread slack notifications can bring your mood down. To help, develop a system so you can handle this flow of messages and help develop a workplace culture that respects other people's time and priorities.

1. When you get a notification, decide immediately how you will deal with it. If it's a quick task, get it done right away. If it's a larger task, write it down to take care of later.

2. Do your best to keep your unread messages at 0. If you can't give someone what they ask for immediately, send a quick response that you will get to it in the future.

3. Mute Slack/Teams channels that are not useful to you. For example, there will often be channels for general chatting and lighthearted banter. If you find those annoying or distracting, turn off their notifications.

4. Look for settings to hide message contents on your phone or laptop. You'll get the notification to know you have a message, but not knowing the contents of the message can keep you focused on your current task.

5. Consider setting up a designated focus time within your team. This is dedicated time where you will do work alone and when your team knows to leave you alone.

6. Ask your coworkers how they deal with emails/Slack/Teams. Do they have a strategy for dealing with them all?

7. If you feel like these platforms are hindering your productivity, talk with your boss. They might be able to influence your team's culture around messaging, or at the very least offer some advice on how to manage better.

8. Have a meeting with your team members about what the ground rules are for messaging apps. Does every message need to be replied to immediately? Is it okay to message during off work hours? What are expectations for replies? Make sure everyone is on the same page

9. Research messaging etiquette online. Hundreds of people have written blogs and Reddit posts about how to manage your messages and notifications.

10. Talk to friends who work at different companies. See if they do anything differently that you can apply in your own company.

11. Work with a coach to develop strategies for managing messages.

12. Read *Getting Things Done* by David Allen, which outlines a basic flow for moving from email or message to getting the required task done (See the For Further Reading section).

See Also:
Challenge 11: Social Media at Work
Challenge 40: Difficulty Working from Home
Challenge 41: Want to Improve Your Time Management
Challenge 70: Colleagues Don't Respect Boundaries/Requests

Take Action: Put your phone and laptop on silent or vibrate mode. Having less noise in your life can help you concentrate.

Challenge 40: Difficulty Working From Home

Whether you think remote work is the future or you're stuck at home because of office pandemic closures, working from home is becoming a part of regular white-collar work. With how quickly this trend has taken the world, many people are still trying to figure out how to navigate this new way of working. Here are some ideas to on how you can tackle the common issues one faces when moving from the office to the home.

1. Create a designated "work only" space. This can be a separate room, a designated corner of the living room, or even a desk that's only for work.
2. Have something to separate work time and home time. For example, you can dress up like you're going to work, then change into loungewear when you are done for the day.
3. Use different computers for work and personal use. This can prevent you from getting distracted by work emails while you're messaging friends or watching videos.
4. Have a routine. This can help if you have trouble starting or stopping work. Consider going for a walk around the block to begin your day, then walking back around when you're done.
5. If you have roommates, let them know when you need alone time to take meetings or focus on work.
6. If your roommates also work from home, negotiate the space. You and your roommates may like working in the same room, or you may want to have separate rooms or areas for each person.
7. Consider renting a coworking space. This is local office space where remote workers commute to for their work.

Some companies provide a work from home stipend that can help pay for a coworking space.

8. If you are in a noisy environment, get noise cancelling headphones

9. Make sure you're getting social interaction somehow. This can include meeting up with friends, attending clubs, or having calls with your loved ones.

10. Consider having productivity calls with coworkers. Simply get on a call with a coworker while you both quietly do your work and check in periodically. This can help if you have trouble working alone.

11. Obtain a coach who can help you figure out how to work remotely.

See Also:
Challenge 28: Should I Work Remotely?
Challenge 33: Hard to Finish Tasks
Challenge 41: Want to Improve Your Time Management
Challenge 44: How to Build Good Habits

Take Action: Research working from home on forums and podcasts. There is no one-size-fits-all solution for working from home. Find the bits that might work for you.

Challenge 41: Want to Improve Time Management

Has this ever happened to you: You start the day off bright and early with a long list of what you're going to get done. Before you know it, it's already 5pm and you're not even close to the end of the list! It's okay to want to do a lot (it's a sign that you're driven and ambitious). However, Rome wasn't built in a day, so don't expect to reach your dreams immediately either. Time is a resource. Like how you spend your money resources on food or wood/concrete resources to build a house, you must spend your limited time resources wisely.

1. Before your day begins, decide the one or two things that need to be done. Make a plan to complete them. Some people like to do this first thing in the morning; others plan tomorrow's goals at the end of the previous workday.
2. Accommodate for your working style. Some people prefer working in 5-10 minute bursts, whereas others need longer 30-40 minute blocks to make progress. Consider if you are a morning or night person, and schedule harder tasks for when you have more energy.
3. Factor in break time when planning your day. This can be time where you can goof off or do an easy activity like clearing your notifications.
4. Consider having a work/break system, such as with pomodoro technique, in which you work for 25 minutes, then break for 5. This way, you don't forget to take that important rest.
5. Add events to your calendar app dedicated to getting things done. Use this time as a personal commitment to work.

6. Keep track of when you have meetings. You don't want to spend 5 minutes getting started on work only to then have a meeting 10 minutes later.

7. Remove unnecessary meetings or obligations from your life. A common example of this is pointless meetings at work. Talk diplomatically with your boss about how to make the meeting more effective or ask if you could not attend.

8. Remember that you have a limited amount of time in the day. Don't schedule more work than you can complete.

9. Time management is different from project management. Time management is about the day-to-day, project is completing long term goals. Look in the "See Also" section below for sections about projects.

10. Consider reducing your number of obligations. For example, if you have multiple people asking you for the equivalent of full-time work, ask them if you can take on less work from them.

11. If you are being assigned more work than you can handle in one day, talk about it with your boss.

12. Talk to someone who is good with time management for advice.

See Also:
Challenge 4: Setting Goals and Priorities
Challenge 16: How to Ask for Help
Challenge 33: Hard-to-Finish Tasks
Challenge 43: Too Many Projects/Tasks

Take Action: Buy sticky notes or a whiteboard. Use it to keep track of your main goal for each day.

Challenge 42: Want to Improve Your Organization

While taking responsibility at work can further your career and give you a sense of empowerment, it can also be a source of stress and anxiety, especially when you don't know how to organize your projects. Organization is more than just to-do lists and calendars; it's a way to take control of your work. Knowing what needs to get done and how those things will get done will not only give you peace of mind, but also make the projects progress smoothly. Note that a project is different from a task. A project refers to work with a set end goal that has multiple parts. Tasks are usually self-contained and can be completed in 1-2 days.

1. Keep a list of what needs to be done for a project. The list for simple projects can just be a plain word document. A more complicated project can be handled with dedicated management software.

2. Make a timeline for when the tasks in a project should be completed. The timeline doesn't have to be perfect, just give you an idea of when you'll be done. It's better to have a timeline you can change later than no timeline at all.

3. Determine the minimum requirements for the project and prioritize them in your task list and timeline. For a product, these are usually the core features you need to launch.

4. Keep all important work information in one place, such as a cloud drive folder or a master document. Instead of having to peruse hundreds of emails or slack messages for information, you'll know exactly where to find it.

5. Schedule external meetings and orders well in advance. People outside of the project are often the biggest bottlenecks for completing a project on time.

6.   Make time to update your task list and project timeline as requirements and resources change. Don't expect to capture all the necessary information on the first go-around.
7.   Talk to your boss or other project stakeholders about what is important in the project and how to best prioritize.
8.   Talk to teammates and colleagues about how reasonable your proposed plan is. The people who will best know how easy or how long a task will take are the people who do the work.
9.   Ask a coach or mentor for feedback on your plan. They will know you and what you are capable of – and how to help you grow!
10.   Meet with someone who is good at organizing to develop a project plan. Ask about how they stay organized and what suggestions they have.

See Also:
Challenge 4: Setting Goals and Priorities
Challenge 5: Making Progress on Goals
Challenge 45: Managing Multiple Responsibilities
Challenge 85: Don't Have Resources to Complete Work

Take Action: Write down the most important thing that needs to be get done right now. Create a plan for getting that task done.

Challenge 43: Too Many Projects/Tasks

Do you feel overwhelmed by a massive barrage of tasks? Are you juggling 2 or 3 or even more projects at once? Do you worry about whether you can keep up with it all? You need to figure out exactly what is required of you, which work is most important, and get help if you need it.

1. Determine project due dates, including midway and final dates. Prioritize tasks that are required soon and set aside time in the future for tasks due later.
2. Discuss with your boss or coworkers which work is the most urgent. This information will help you prioritize.
3. See if there's any work that is optional or which can be delayed. Many times, tasks that feel important are not actually required.
4. Make a plan. Create a timeline of when you will get things done. This will help give you peace of mind in getting the tasks done.
5. Figure out what work requires a lot of effort and what does not. It's okay if an email to a coworker is not your finest writing. Instead, put more energy towards an important task, like preparing a presentation to your project stakeholders.
6. Know your limits. Can you put in the extra hours to meet the additional workload? Or do you have other responsibilities outside of work? These limits will help you plan.
7. Ask your boss or stakeholders for additional time. Here, having a plan or timeline can help you make the case for why that additional time is necessary.
8. Consider reaching out to coworkers to ask for additional help. Often a project is a team effort, and your team should pick up where you need help.

9. Have a frank discussion with your boss about what you are capable of doing. Even for talented employees, there is a limit to what is a reasonable workload.
10. Talk with a mentor about how they have gotten through times like this in their career.
11. Work with a coach on organizing and prioritizing your projects and tasks
12. Observe the company culture. If people are expected to do a lot of work at your company without receiving any help, your situation may not be unique. Ideally, your company or team should be giving you the necessary resources to complete your work.
13. If this level of work is too much for you, consider that this company or position might not right for you.

See Also:
Challenge 2: Setting Boundaries
Challenge 46: Difficulty Saying No
Challenge 58: Colleague Doesn't Contribute
Challenge 84: Don't Feel Supported by Boss
Challenge 85: Don't Have Resources to Complete Work

Take Action: Write down everything you need to do. Even if the list is 50 items long, having it all in one place makes the end feel tangible.

Challenge 44. How to Build Good Habits

We all know what habits are good. We know that eating healthy foods, exercising, getting work done, and reaching out to friends are good. However, actually making these activities a habit is much harder than just knowing that you should do them. You need a system which makes the habit as easy as can be, and to also check in with your progress over time.

1. Ask why do you want to build the habit? Keep your "why" written down or in the back of your mind when you are unsure about whether the habit is worth building.
2. Make sure your desired new habit is worth it. Some things (like exercise or time with loved ones) are intrinsically valuable. However, it doesn't make sense try to become an early bird if you know you work better at night.
3. Focus on building one habit at a time. Trying to change too much about yourself all at once can lead to confusion and burnout, especially if this is your first time building a new habit.
4. Make the habit small and easily measurable. Something like, "write one page of my novel every day after work".
5. Keep track of your progress. This can be a small journal or note app. Simply write the date and whether or not you did the habit. Track your progress until the habit is ingrained and you feel like tracking is no longer helpful. This usually takes 3-4 weeks of doing the habit every day.
6. Tie the habit to a particular space or device. For example, have a corner of your living room dedicated to making music or a laptop dedicated to writing.
7. Set reminders with your phone alarm or calendar app to remind you to do the habit.

8. Reflect at regular intervals about how the habit is going. If you are struggling with keeping up the habit, consider switching up how you approach it.

9. Remember that changing behavior as an adult is very hard. Many adults simply do not change their lifestyle or habits throughout their entire life. But with your drive and persistence, you can make it happen.

10. Talk to friends or coworkers about their experience and attempts with setting habits for themselves.

11. Get an accountability buddy. This is someone who you check in with every day or week to see how you are doing with your habit.

12. Work with a coach to create a habit-building plan.

13. For more on habit building, read *Triggers: Creating Behavior That Lasts–Becoming the Person You Want to Be* by Marshall Goldsmith (See the For Further Reading section).

See Also:
Challenge 6: How to Evaluate Yourself
Challenge 16: How to Ask for Help
Challenge 33: Hard-to-Finish Tasks
Challenge 42: Want to Improve Your Organization

Take Action: Put a reminder sticky-note on your desk or bed side for your habit. Some place you see every day so you don't forget.

Challenge 45: Managing Multiple Responsibilities

If you're full of energy and ambition, you might find it hard to stick to only one or two ambitions at a time. So, you take on additional responsibilities, be it more work at your day job or side hustles. While wearing many hats can be fun and rewarding, it requires additional management of tasks and checking in to make sure that you're getting your main responsibilities done right.

1. Set aside some time every day to focus on each of your obligations.

2. Keep track of what work you need to do for each one of your responsibilities. This can be a formal to-do list or a notebook. A list can be very helpful if you need to jump between different kinds of work frequently.

3. Keep a calendar to remember appointments and prevent scheduling conflicts.

4. Take responsibilities that complement each other or for which you can "double dip." For example, if you are managing a team, a good secondary responsibility would be to interview potential candidates for the team. Or if you are attending a training, offer to share that training with your colleagues so you get credit for both.

5. While having a lot of different responsibilities can be fun, be aware of your limits and don't burn yourself out.

6. Get better at saying no. Know what responsibilities are important and which ones are not; develop discernment.

7. Check in with your boss and supervisor regularly to make sure that your multiple obligations are not interfering with each other.

8. Work with a mentor to manage your different responsibilities

9. Get a coach to determine plans and strategies for managing your responsibilities.

10. If you are worried about burnout or the negative effects of having too many responsibilities, work with a therapist or counselor.

See Also:
Challenge 27: Wanting Multiple Jobs or Side Hustles
Challenge 42: Want to Improve Your Organization
Challenge 43: Too Many Projects/Tasks

Take Action: Write down all the hats you want to wear and what your responsibilities are for each of those hats. Review your system for organizing your time to ensure you can complete everything you want to finish.

Challenge 46: Difficulty Saying No

Although it's just one word, saying no is not always that simple. We may feel coerced into saying yes to avoid conflict or to make ourselves look like a hard worker. Yet, saying yes all the time can lead to overloading yourself with work. To help, determine what things you can say no to and make the act easier through practice.

1. Say no to lower priority tasks. For example, an ask from your boss is more important than a favor for a coworker.
2. Know your work responsibilities according to your job description. You shouldn't have to do more than you were hired for. While the occasional task is fine, if someone makes you do extra work often, tell them that's not your responsibility.
3. Try delaying your answer. Respond with "When do you need an answer?" Often, you don't have to say yes or no right away.
4. Think of alternatives to a hard yes or no, like "I can't do all of it, but I can help with this part," or "I know someone who'd be a great help with that."
5. Practice saying no with friends or family.
6. Consider saying no over email or message if saying it face-to-face is difficult.
7. Imagine what will happen if you say no. Telling a coworker once that you can't help likely will not lead to any issues.
8. If you repeatedly take on extra work, consider talking about it with your boss. They can help you get less work assigned or possibly give you a raise to compensate.
9. It's okay to change your yes to a no if something urgent comes up.
10. If you're asked about something optional, like a work party, you can say "no" without explanation.

11. If you are asked to do something illegal or if you feel unsafe saying no, talk to your boss or Human Resources. This is not okay.

See Also:
Challenge 8: When and How to Obtain a Coach
Challenge 13: How to Have Difficult Conversations
Challenge 51: Difficulty Speaking in Public
Challenge 61: Colleague are Difficult to Approach

Take Action: Think about an ask that you should always say "no" to.

Challenge 47: Bored at Work

For many people, their dream job is one where every day is full of exciting or interesting problems to work on. If that's you, there's nothing worse than a boring job; work that feels like you're doing the same thing over and over again. If you're at a boring job or if you're just in a slow spell, there are ways to make tasks a bit more interesting. Ask your boss for different assignments. Novelty is a good short-term solution to boredom.

1. Keep your eye on the prize. Acknowledge that sometimes working towards your goals will involve some boring parts.
2. Listen to a podcast or audiobook while doing the boring work. This is good for labor work or repetitive tasks.
3. Find a way to push yourself within your current responsibilities. Try to complete more work than last week, do it faster, or do it in a different style.
4. Look for excitement outside of work. You can join interesting clubs, travel, or spend time with friends and family. Even if work is boring, at least you'll have something to look forward to after hours.
5. Ask colleagues if they are working on anything interesting. They may even ask you to get involved with something exciting!
6. Create challenges with other teammates so the boring work becomes more of a game.
7. Ask other teams if they need help with anything. Working with a different team can be a good opportunity to network and try something new.
8. If the boredom persists for a long time, consider discussing new or different responsibilities with your boss, or consider a transfer to a new team within your company.

9. If you think your company is no longer interesting, this company may no longer be right for you.

10. If you find yourself bored across multiple jobs and companies, talk about your experience with a therapist or career coach. They can help you identify ongoing problems.

See Also:
Challenge 1: Determining Your Values
Challenge 24: You Think It's Time to Move On
Challenge 37: Feel Negative about Work
Challenge 56: Meetings are Frustrating

Take Action: Write down one thing you see other people do at your company which you'd be interested in trying.

Challenge 48: Shy/Introverted

For those of us that are shy or introverted, the meetings and talks required of the modern workplace can be overwhelming. You're not alone! At least half of the U.S. population is introverted, which describes someone who is predominantly focused on their own thoughts and feelings. Even if that describes you, there are ways to make your interaction style work inside the workplace.

1. Take note of situations where being an introvert holds you back. It may only be in certain meetings or when you're with certain people. Address those situations individually.

2. Set up an in-person or virtual meeting with people one-on-one or in smaller groups. You might find it easier to talk with fewer people in the room.

3. Make a list of what you need to talk about before a meeting. With this list, you can focus on finding time to speak and not worry about what you need to say.

4. Practice what you want to say with friends, family, or trusted colleagues. You can also practice what you want to say in front of a mirror. Imagine you're talking to the person or in the middle of a meeting. This can make it easier for you to speak.

5. Talk to the person running the meeting beforehand. Ask them to call on you to speak, so you can expect when you'll be able to start talking.

6. Consider emailing your ideas to the team after the meeting. You can take your time to word it properly and don't have to worry about stepping over other voices.

7. Ask coworkers if they feel like you're too quiet or shy. Your introversion may not be as big of a deal as you originally thought.

8. If you're collaborating on a project, ask a more outgoing colleague to handle speaking up at meetings or discussions.

9. Consider attending your local Toastmasters group. Toastmasters help people improve their comfort in public speaking, including impromptu speaking.

10. Work with a coach to build strategies on how to work with your introversion.

11. Talk to a therapist about what is making you shy and possible solutions.

12. Read *Quiet: The Power of Introverts in a World that Can't Stop Talking* by Susan Cain (See the For Further Reading section).

See Also:
Challenge 10: Building Relationships with Colleagues
Challenge 32: You Want to Increase Your Influence
Challenge 51: Difficulty Speaking in Public
Challenge 61: Colleague are Difficult to Approach

Take Action: Pick one suggestion, such as email or one-on-one meetings, that is more comfortable for you and commit to trying it this week.

Challenge 49: Overly Concerned about Other's Feelings

Relationships are a key part of work. We have our bosses to report to and rely on our coworkers for assistance. But it can be difficult when we are constantly unsure about what those people are thinking of. The solution is feedback and practice. Get feedback on how other people view your words and actions. Practice getting that feedback.

1. Be direct; ask someone else what they think about you. Don't let your mind imagine things that other people don't really feel.

2. Ask your boss or someone you trust what the general office attitude towards you is.

3. If you're not sure how you may come across to others, ask a trusted coworker to be a sounding board. Say, "Can I run something by you before speaking to the rest of the team?".

4. Focus on doing your work well and on time. People are unlikely to be upset with you if are a good worker.

5. Limit words like "sorry" or "thank you" to once per interaction. Over-apologizing can be off-putting and unhelpful.

6. Consider asking "Is it okay if I say something? I don't know if it'll come off okay." This is a temporary solution but can get you started with emotional sensitivity.

7. Before speaking up, first identify your own feelings on the subject. This can help you rationalize the feelings of others and how they might respond.

8. Consider how important the feelings of this person are. Your boss' feelings are much more important than a random person from another department.

9. Remember that understanding emotions is difficult. It can take a lot of work, but if you work at it, you will notice improvements in both your work and personal life.
10. You might consider getting a coach or a therapist to help with your concerns.
11. Consider if you are acting in accordance with the values of your team or company. Straying from those values can create tension with others.

See Also:
Challenge 9: When and How to Obtain a Therapist
Challenge 37: Feel Negative about Work
Challenge 44: How to Build Good Habits

Take Action: Create a list of people you can talk about these feelings with and start connecting.

Challenge 50: Difficult to Accept Praise

Receiving praise can be an incredible and validating experience. But for many people, it can be nerve-wracking, bringing out their most embarrassing tics and habits. There's nothing wrong with being a bit awkward if you respond gracefully and respectfully towards the compliment.

1. Just say "Thank You." Most of the time, your response to praise doesn't have to be complicated.
2. Keep your reply sincere. While you should at least say "Thank you," don't feel obligated to say more about praise you don't care about.
3. Determine if praise is the kind of feedback you would like. If you would rather get something else, like constructive criticism, ask for it.
4. Keep track of who praises you and for what. You can reach out to these people when you need help in the future.
5. Don't minimize the praise like "Oh it wasn't much." At best you'll come off as humble, but at worst you'll make the other person feel invalidated.
6. Imagine what your ideal reaction would be to praise. Practice giving that response in front of a mirror or with a friend.
7. If you don't have the energy to respond to everyone, prioritize the people you trust or appreciate the most.
8. Pay attention to how other people accept praise. See if they do something you could copy.
9. It's okay to get nervous while receiving compliments. You could even make a joke about how nervous you are in conversation. The other people should be understanding.
10. If you think your work does not deserve praise, consider changing how you work. This can be taking on more

       meaningful projects or putting more effort into what you're already doing.

11.   Consider if you only get praised for work that you don't care about. This may be a sign that your company's culture is not a good fit for you.

12.   Talk to a trusted person, like a mentor, friend, or coach, about your issues.

See Also:
Challenge 9: When and How to Obtain a Therapist
Challenge 10: Building Relationships with Colleagues
Challenge 48: Shy/Introverted

Take Action: Identify one bad habit you have about receiving praise and develop a plan for dealing with it.

Challenge 51: Difficulty Speaking in Public

Have you ever frozen up while giving a speech or presentation? Does the mere idea of speaking in front of an audience send shivers down your spine? That means you, like many people, get nervous about public speaking. The best way to work through this difficulty is to practice. And practice some more. Get some feedback from coworkers or friends. Then do more practice.

1. Create an outline of your talking points. Having an outline can help you focus less on what you're going to say and more on the speaking itself.
2. Keep your speech or presentation to 1-3 main points. This makes it easier both for your audience to follow along and for you to memorize your speech.
3. Determine what your key takeaway is. What is the one thing you want your audience to learn, feel, or do after hearing your speech?
4. If your presentation has a question-and-answer session, make a list of possible questions and practice answering them.
5. Practice speaking in front of a mirror.
6. Record yourself speaking with your phone or laptop. Then, listen over the recording and take note of what you can improve on.
7. Ask friends or family if you can practice in front of them. Even if they don't have any feedback, having a live audience can make practice feel more like the real deal.
8. Make a list of tics or bad habits you are worried about when speaking. Think of ways to counter those habits.
9. Ask someone who is good at public speaking for advice on how to improve.

10. When working with someone else, ask for specific feedback. This can be: How was my volume? Were my points clear? Were you bored with my speech?

11. If your project involves multiple people, consider giving the presentation with a coworker. This way, you are not responsible for 100% of the public speaking.

12. Look for opportunities to practice public speaking at work.

13. Join a local public speaking club such as Toastmasters International. They can provide a warm and supportive environment to practice your public speaking.

14. Work with a public speaking coach to iron out your problems.

See Also:
Challenge 8: When and How to Obtain a Coach
Challenge 48: Shy/Introverted
Challenge 49: Overly Concerned about Other's Feelings

Take Action: Make plans to start practicing your public speaking as soon as you know you have to give a presentation.

Part 4. Colleague Challenges

Challenge 52: Accused of Wrongdoing

Most office talk is idle chit-chat. However, there are times when you may be accused of a serious offense, such as sexual harassment or plagiarism. Regardless of the threat level, keep a cool head and have a plan to handle the situation.

1. Determine what the scope of the accusation is. Is this gossip or a serious accusation that could have legal repercussions?
2. Know your alibi. When people speak against your character or actions, it's important to know what's true.
3. Speak to your boss or another trusted senior person about the matter. Their testimony could be useful in a trial.
4. Consult Human Resources. While they have the company's best interest first, they may be able to assist you.
5. Talk to an attorney about what your legal options are.
6. Don't delete files. This will make you look suspicious.
7. Remember your data from your work devices are permissible in a court of law. Don't keep sensitive information on company-owned devices.
8. Understand that many people will avoid you while the accusations are still in the air. Treat them kindly if coolly.
9. Make sure you have contact with your external support network, be it friends or family. They are valuable both for emotional support and advice.
10. If being at work is stressful, consider taking a leave of absence until the incident ends.

See Also:
Challenge 9: When and How to Obtain a Therapist
Challenge 13: How to Have Difficult Conversations

Challenge 19: Understanding Hierarchy at Work
Challenge 64: Backstabbing

Take Action: Write down your next action to deal with an accusation.

Challenge 53: Hard to Make Small Talk

Small talk: those moments of idle chatter that occur before meetings and at the water cooler. Like them or not, they are a continual presence in work life. If you find yourself struggling at small talk, first consider if being good at small talk is important to you. If so, work on it like any other skill.

1. Ask yourself if small talk matters. You may be able to complete your work and goals without it.
2. Have a goal when approaching small talk. if you want to build a relationship with your coworkers, ask them about their life. If you want to have some fun, just remain kind and respectful.
3. Figure out what your colleagues are into. Ask them questions about their interests and hobbies.
4. To avoid small talk, only speak when spoken to. Don't force yourself to talk more than necessary.
5. Another way to avoid small talk is to minimize one-on-one interactions. With more people, there's less likely to be dead air.
6. Look up a list of "small talk" questions that you can ask colleagues or prepare to answer yourself.
7. Create an "elevator pitch" for when people ask you what you do. This includes your title, team, and regular duties.
8. Read articles from your industry so you have a conversation starter.
9. Reach out to public speaking organizations such as Toastmasters. These clubs provide a safe place to practice talking in a professional setting.
10. Find people who are good at small talk and ask them for advice.
11. Practice small talk with friends or family.

12. Work with a coach on how to improve your small talking abilities.
13. Consider if you don't like small talk because you don't like your coworkers. This could be a sign that this company is not for you.

See Also:
Challenge 10: Building Relationships with Colleagues
Challenge 15: When and How to Have Face-to-Face Conversations
Challenge 61: Colleague are Difficult to Approach

Take Action: Keep your elevator pitch or conversations starters on your person at all times, just in case you need it.

Challenge 54: You Feel Like You're Not Heard

Sometimes, even when we speak or have good ideas, it feels like our words are falling on deaf ears. Your managers and your team should ensure that everyone on the team feels heard and valued, but unfortunately, that doesn't always happen. Here are some suggestions for you to feel more heard and ways to ask for help.

1. Contact people directly via email or messages. Stage the conversation on your own terms.
2. Think about situations where you felt heard. What separates that time from you felt not heard? See if you can recreate those circumstances.
3. Imagine what other people could do to make you feel more heard. Examples include giving affirmations or asking questions. Ask people you trust to do these things, saying "It would help me feel heard if you did them."
4. See if the people around you are getting treated differently than you. Perhaps people who speak up more are more likely to get heard.
5. Discuss this issue with your boss. Ask if they can change their or the team's behavior to help you feel more heard.
6. Consider if only senior people get heard. Sometimes notice comes with status in a company.
7. Look for a friend that matches your intersectionality (race, sexual orientation, gender, background, etc.). Simply knowing someone who is like you can help you feel heard.
8. Join your local Toastmasters club. Toastmasters is an international organization with local clubs that provides a safe environment to grow your speaking ability in corporate environments.

9.   Consider if you have any vocal quirks which may impede how much you are heard. A vocal coach can help you iron these quirks out or develop strategies for living with them.

10. If you have a long-term pattern of feeling unheard, consider working with a therapist to determine if there are any emotional or personal reasons you feel unheard and to address them.

11. Consider that certain teams or meetings (such as large, company-wide meetings) are not conducive to you feeling heard. Adjust your expectations accordingly.

See Also:
Challenge 51: Difficulty Speaking in Public
Challenge 56: Meetings are Frustrating
Challenge 84: Don't Feel Supported by Boss

Take Action: Keep track of all the situations where you feel not heard at work. Identify any patterns between these situations and imagine what you would prefer to happen instead. How can you make that happen?

Challenge 55: Colleagues Frequently Interrupt

Work should be a place where your thoughts and contributions are appreciated. However, sometimes you can be interrupted mid-speaking. How rude! While such occasions are sometimes inevitable, it's a problem if interruptions occur on a regular basis. You can develop strategies for dealing with interruptions and reduce their likelihood.

1. Send important info through an email after a meeting. Interruptions should not stop you from passing along vital information.
2. Make notes of what you want to say before the meeting or conversation. Notes help you focus less on what you need to say and more on actually speaking.
3. After getting interrupted, use a transition to bring the conversation back to your topic, such as, "Good point, and I want to finish before we move on".
4. Consider that you may have a tick or habit that invites interruptions. Let people know that those behaviors are not an invitation to interrupt you.
5. Ask the meeting runner to give the floor back to you after you're interrupted.
6. If there is an agenda, make sure that you are given a time slot and that that time is respected.
7. Speak to the interrupters in private. Ask them to stop interrupting you.
8. Ask your boss for help. They can reach out to the interrupters themselves or intervene on your behalf.
9. Practice speaking with a friend. This can be a safe way to rehearse what you want to say. Your friend can even pretend to interrupt so you are more prepared for when it happens.

10. Identify colleagues who are shy or who don't speak up much. Ask them how they manage when they need to talk.

11. Ask someone who can handle interruptions for advice on how to be more skillful in conversations.

12. If you are not confident speaking, consider finding a local Toastmasters organization. Toastmasters is an international organization with local chapters designed to build your comfort speaking in formal settings.

13. Consider working with a coach to deal with interrupters or to iron out habits that welcome it.

See Also:
Challenge 8: When and How to Obtain a Coach
Challenge 51: Difficulty Speaking in Public
Challenge 54: You Feel Like You're Not Heard
Challenge 68: Colleagues are Bigoted or Hostile

Take Action: Imagine being interrupted by someone else, and then think about how you would respond in a constructive manner.

Challenge 56: Meetings are Frustrating

Nobody likes long boring meetings where you sit still for hours upon hours while listening to people drone on about information that is not relevant to your work. Worse still, there are times when you're supposed to be learning critical information, but the group ends up getting derailed! Meetings can be a useful tool for spreading for information, but they can easily be mismanaged or inefficient. Do your part to keep them running smoothly and cut out the fat.

1. Ask if there is a meeting agenda or make one yourself. Use this to guide the meeting or to gauge your understanding of the meeting's purpose.
2. Keep the meeting small and down to what's required. If a conversation only needs 3 team members present, don't force others to attend and email the results out if need be.
3. Take notes during the meeting. You don't need to write down everything, but paying attention to what is important or not can keep you alert throughout the meeting.
4. If you're the meeting runner, make sure it starts and ends on time. If meetings run over, consider scheduling more time or shrinking the agenda.
5. Have the meeting runner call on people instead of waiting for volunteers. This can avoid awkward waiting for someone to start speaking.
6. When someone goes off topic, gently remind them to stay on agenda. If you lack authority, get a boss or trusted senior to back you up when you call the meeting to order.
7. At the end of a meeting, consider ways to improve the next meeting.
8. Consider if your attendance is necessary for the meeting. If not, ask the meeting runner if you can skip it.

9. Determine if your attention is necessary. If not, you can multitask or take care of errands like checking email while passively listening.
10. If someone is at the meeting who has nothing to contribute, ask the meeting runner if they must be there. Fewer people means shorter meetings and fewer chances to get off topic.
11. Rotate the boring tasks like taking notes so no one is stuck doing the same thing repeatedly.

See Also:
Challenge 4: Setting Goals and Priorities
Challenge 15: When and How to Have Face-to-Face Conversations
Challenge 46: Difficulty Saying No
Challenge 47: Bored at Work

Take Action: Is the problem with your meeting that you aren't getting enough value from them or that they are not run well?

Challenge 57: Annoying Office Mate

No matter how courteous or kind or understanding you are, there is usually one person who manages to push your buttons. That's okay; you don't have to like everyone at work. But you do have to get along. Here's some suggestions on how.

1.   Talk to the person about what's annoying you. For small things (like lip smacking), the person might not even be aware they are doing it.

2.   Know the office rules and use them when talking to the person. For example, if there is a rule to not play loud music and the person is blasting their speakers, remind them of that rule.

3.   Purchase headphones. If your office allows them, headphones can drown out whatever noise your coworker is making.

4.   Find a place to work far away from this person. This can prevent tension from building between you and them.

5.   Work in the office when the annoying person is not there. Many offices are open a few hours before and after most people show up.

6.   Avoid conversations involving this person to reduce your exposure to them. There will be other water cooler opportunities to talk to your coworkers.

7.   If you need to talk to this person, bring a friend so you're not alone. When they start being bothersome, have your friend bring the conversation back on track.

8.   Ask your other colleagues diplomatically if this person is annoying them too. If they agree, you have a stronger case to confront this person or to discuss with your boss or Human Resources.

9.   Consider if the thing annoying you is within the person's control. Some people have conditions which they don't

have control over. In those cases, it's on you to be understanding and respectful.

10. If their annoying behavior is dangerous to your health, like bringing in peanut butter when you have a nut allergy, speak with Human Resources.

11. If you feel comfortable, talk with your boss about the annoying behaviors. Keep the focus on the actions and how they affect you, not on the person. Your boss may be able to help.

12. Discuss strategies on how to deal with this person with a coach.

See Also:
Challenge 2: Setting Boundaries
Challenge 13: How to Have Difficult Conversations
Challenge 55: Colleagues Frequently Interrupt

Take Action: Write down exactly what is annoying you and brainstorm ideas on how to cope.

Challenge 58: Colleague Doesn't Contribute

Often, the projects you work on are too large to handle alone, requiring the contributions of multiple people. Ideally, the work is split so that each person works their fair share. But, if one or more colleagues don't contribute, it can put the whole project at risk. When this happens, figure out what the problem is and find ways to proceed.

1. Make sure everyone on the team is clear about each person's responsibilities. They may be unsure or mistaken about what they must do, leaving important work undone.

2. Set boundaries for what you're willing to do. You may be okay doing a task for another coworker or are not okay at all. Remember that other people's tasks should not be your responsibility.

3. Have a discussion with a colleague who might not be pulling their weight. There might be a personal reason as to why they can't contribute. Be kind.

4. See if there are other ways your colleague can contribute which better fits them. It could be that the work is a bad match or they have a problem outside of work that is affecting them.

5. Ask your colleague if they need help. Perhaps they're missing critical information or expertise.

6. If your colleague always dodges your questions, consider asking them about the project during meetings or group settings.

7. Send reminders via email or message about their work. They might just be forgetful.

8. Talk with your boss about their lack of contributing. Your boss may be able to give you more time or more resources to make up for it.

9. If the colleague is known for not contributing, take this into account when planning projects and timelines.
10. Remember that life can bring the unexpected. A colleague who normally contributes a lot may suddenly not be able to do much if they or a family member get sick. To an extent, you will have to learn to roll with the punches.
11. If your company culture does not care about their lack of work, consider if this company is right for you.

See Also:
Challenge 13: How to Have Difficult Conversations
Challenge 16: How to Ask for Help
Challenge 42: Want to Improve Your Organization
Challenge 85: Don't Have Resources to Complete Work
Challenge 93: Company Culture Is Not Supportive

Take Action: Check with the project manager to ensure that the outcome of the project does not depend entirely on one person. Human beings are not machines.

Challenge 59: Colleague Takes Credit for Your Work

You work long and hard at a project or a task, but then once it's all said and done, someone else takes credit for what you've done! Outrageous! Make sure your boss and colleagues know who was really responsible and take precautionary steps to ensure that this does not happen again.

1. Let your colleague know that they stole your credit. They may be unaware that their actions were rude to you.

2. Stay away from people known for stealing credit. You can look out for them or diplomatically ask your boss or trusted colleagues who those people might be.

3. Make sure responsibilities are clearly defined at the beginning of the project. Once the project is completed, you can look back at the plan to assign proper credit.

4. Keep notes on who is doing what as the project progresses. When someone says they did your work, you could provide a rebuttal.

5. Build relationships with your colleagues. People are less likely to steal your credit or be rude to you if they feel like they know you.

6. Talk to your boss about the credit being stolen. They may be able to correct the error or give you the proper reward.

7. Don't wait until the end of the project to discuss your concerns about credit and responsibilities. Talk about what you're working on with your coworkers as the project progresses. This will make it harder for someone to step in at the last second and steal your credit.

8. Open a discussion with your boss and your coworkers about how credit should be given out. Make sure everyone is on the same page.

9. If feeling taken advantage of feels like a pattern across your life, consider talking to a therapist about the causes and solutions.

10. If the credit stealer faces no repercussions, consider that this company may not be right for you. Remember, you deserve credit for your hard work.

See Also:
Challenge 13: How to Have Difficult Conversations
Challenge 60: Colleagues are Extremely Competitive
Challenge 64: Backstabbing
Challenge 84: Don't Feel Supported by Boss

Take Action: Write down a list of your personal achievements. If you don't get your deserved acknowledgement, at least know for yourself what you have done.

Challenge 60: Colleagues are Extremely Competitive

Competition can motivate you to grow and develop; competition can also stress you out and make you very uncomfortable. If the level of competition in your work team is not a right fit for you, there are strategies to either work around the competitiveness or increase your ability to work in such an environment.

1. Consider being a neutral party. Instead of trying to get ahead, help whoever needs it.
2. Grow your abilities and knowledge through training and projects so you can keep up with your more competitive colleagues.
3. Determine how promotions, raises, bonuses are handled in your team or company. This information can help you prioritize which competitions may be worth your time.
4. Determine if joining the competition is healthy for you. For some, competition can be a healthy motivator. For others, competition can be an all-consuming force. Or you can be somewhere in between. Where do you land?
5. Consider that the competition may reflect cultural differences. Behavior you view as competitive can see as normal by others.
6. Figure out if not being competitive will hurt you. If staying out does not impact your performance reviews or work, you can sit on the side.
7. Ask a trusted competitive colleague for advice in this situation.
8. Talk your boss about how important competition is for your job duties. Don't do what you don't have to.
9. Speak to someone outside your work for their thoughts and how well competition could work for you.
10. Work with a coach to increase your ability to compete.

11. If the competitive dynamic does not work for you, look for a transfer to a different team.
12. Observe if competitive behavior is common amongst everyone within your company. If so, this may be a sign that this company is not right for you.

See Also:
Challenge 1: Determining Your Values
Challenge 2: Setting Boundaries
Challenge 37: Feel Negative about Work
Challenge 91: Company Culture is Overly Competitive
Challenge 93: Company Culture Is Not Supportive

Take Action: What skills do you feel confident and capable with? Use this to your advantage.

Challenge 61: Colleagues are Difficult to Approach

Sometimes the office culture is that people don't approach each other. This is even more difficult when many coworkers work from home. Sometimes people just don't seem friendly and approachable. Regardless of the reason, sometimes you need to talk to someone and it's hard. And that's okay. You can prepare yourself for the encounter or find alternatives to a regular conversation.

1. Instead of talking to them, send them an email or Slack message. This technique is especially good if the topic does not require a full-on conversation.
2. Leave a note on your colleague's desk about the topic or ask them to talk to you when they have time. Let them come to you when it works for them.
3. Go over what you want to say before approaching them. Being assured of what you want can make you less nervous.
4. Consider if it's necessary to reach out to them. For example, if you want help with a task, it may be easier to get it done yourself than talk to someone else.
5. Practice speaking in front of a mirror or to a friend. This is not the same as talking to a person, but is still good practice.
6. Talk to your boss about the problem. They may be able to give you good advice or set up situations to talk with this colleague.
7. Consider approaching your colleague during a meeting. Having the approach be part of a larger conversation can make it easier.
8. Ask someone who is easier to approach to reach out on your behalf. Note that this is a temporary solution.

9. Work with a coach on how to tackle this problem.
10. Consider joining your local chapter of Toastmasters International. Meetings typically provide an impromptu speaking session where you can practice speaking off the cuff in a professional setting.

See Also:
Challenge 8: When and How to Obtain a Coach
Challenge 15: When and How to Have Face-to-Face
  Conversations
Challenge 51: Difficulty Speaking in Public

Take Action: Determine what about your colleague makes it hard for you to approach them. What are ways to be more successful with this colleague?

Challenge 62: Colleagues are Difficult to Contact

Sometimes, no matter how much you email or message a colleague, they simply fail to respond. This can be incredibly frustrating, especially when the other person is vital to your current task. There are various approaches you can take to solving this problem, including setting up meetings or asking others to contact on your behalf.

1. Leave a polite note on their desk asking them to reach out to you or put the message itself on the note.
2. Send a reminder email. Sometimes people simply forget that about what you told them or forget to respond. Don't take it personally.
3. Try to catch the colleague before or after meetings. It may be easier to chat with them in that environment.
4. Consider establishing a regular round robin or standing meeting where your team or coworkers give everyone updates. This can be useful for the person you are trying to contact in addition to yourself.
5. Ask someone who works with this colleague often to relay the message on your behalf.
6. Talk to your boss about this hard-to-contact colleague. Ask them for suggestions on how to get a response. Your boss can tell the colleague for you or remind them to respond.
7. Have a diplomatic conversation with your other coworkers about this person. Ask if they have any tips for contacting them. There may be a certain time of day where they are more responsive, or other similar tricks.
8. If many of your colleagues are slow to respond in general, discuss this issue with your boss. Problems concerning

your whole team should be handled by the person in charge.

9. Ask your mentor how they deal with difficult to contact colleagues.

10. If this issue persists in your company, consider that this company is not right for you and start looking elsewhere.

See Also:
Challenge 10: Building Relationships with Colleagues
Challenge 35: Feel Isolated
Challenge 39: Can't Manage Emails/Slack/Teams

Take Action: Keep track of who you need to contact and what you need to contact them about. Even if they don't respond, you won't forget with the list.

Challenge 63: Colleagues are Overly/Insufficiently Social

Do your coworkers never stop talking? Or do you have the opposite problem where your coworkers feel like complete strangers? Regardless, making sure your professional social needs are met is important part of company fit. If you feel like your colleagues are too social or not social enough, there are some steps to take to change that.

1. Determine how much social interaction you want. Do you like having the occasional pleasant interaction? Would you prefer to not see your coworkers unless it's work related?

2. Block off focus time for yourself. You can ask your coworkers to not bother you from 10am to 11am (or whatever time) every day. If your boss asks why, say that having the dedicated time makes you more productive. Be open to feedback (such as changing the time to one more convenient for your boss or coworkers).

3. Find a spot in the office where you are unlikely to be interrupted by coworkers.

4. If someone approaches you with something not urgent, say "Thanks for talking to me, but I'm in the middle of something right now. Can we talk about this later?"

5. Come into the office at hours when there are not a lot of people around.

6. If you'd like to see your coworkers more often, schedule one on one meetings with them. You don't have to wait for opportunities to arise spontaneously!

7. Discuss with boss and coworkers about setting up team happy hours or other laid back social engagements. Try to make it a regular thing.

8. Ask coworkers if they would like to hang out more or have more interactions. This could be as simple as working at the same table in the office.
9. Ask Human Resources or company event organizers if they have any social gatherings planned, such as an intermural sports league. This can be a fun way to get to know people.
10. Ask friends in other companies how they manage socializing.
11. Develop strategies with a coach on how to increase or decrease your socializations at work.

See Also:
Challenge 2: Setting Boundaries
Challenge 5: Making Progress on Goals
Challenge 7: When and How to Obtain a Mentor
Challenge 10: Building Relationships with Colleagues
Challenge 53: Hard to Make Small Talk

Take Action: Bring up your interest in socializing to someone you trust within the company, be it a boss or a coworker.

Challenge 64. Backstabbing

Backstabbing is when someone seems to be supportive of you but is actually undermining and criticizing you behind the scenes. This can be incredibly frustrating, especially when you need help for a project or promotion. When you encounter someone like this, do your best to minimize what damage they can cause.

1. Be careful with personal and/or sensitive information. Many times, sharing that information is not for your job and can be a liability around a backstabber.
2. Pay attention to when you are in the vicinity of the backstabber. At those times, avoid sharing information that can be used against you.
3. Think about what the backstabber wants. Use this info to determine what things should be kept away from them.
4. Gather proof of the backstabber's misdeeds: have the receipts. This can be used in a discussion with other coworkers, management, or HR
5. Look for ways to limit working with the backstabber. For example, when you need advice on a topic familiar to the backstabber, reach out to another colleague with similar experience instead.
6. Discuss the backstabber's actions diplomatically with coworkers. See if others have the same experiences as you do. Ask how they manage it.
7. Have a discussion with the backstabber. While confrontation may be difficult, the issue may just be a simple misunderstanding.
8. Talk to someone you trust outside of work for their opinion.
9. Consider transferring to another team within your company.

10. Ask around your company to see if backstabbing is part of the culture. If so, consider that this company might not be for you.

See Also:
Challenge 9: When and How to Obtain a Therapist
Challenge 16: How to Ask for Help
Challenge 65: How Much Personal Information Do I Share with Colleagues?
Challenge 93: Company Culture Is Not Supportive

Take Action: Diplomatically mention the backstabber's actions to a trusted colleague and ask for advice. Having at least one other person on your team know about them can help in the future.

Challenge 65: How Much Personal Information Do I Share with Colleagues?

We all know there is a difference between what you can talk about at work vs. outside of work. However, the line between those two is different depending on your personal comfort and your work environment. Figuring out how much personal information to share is about understanding the overlap between those two forces.

1. Identify personal boundaries. Do you feel comfortable talking about family? What about what you did over the weekend? Hobbies, interests? Avoid crossing those lines if you can.
2. If you're unsure about personal boundaries, start by keeping discussions strictly to work-related topics. From there, you can share more in the future.
3. Pay attention to what information your coworkers are sharing. Don't share more than what they are.
4. Keep track of responses to your personal information. If people are disinterested or weirded out, take that as a sign of oversharing.
5. Start small and build up. Begin with a detail about the weather or plans after work. As time goes on, you can talk about larger things like family and outside ambitions.
6. Talk yourself up about non-personal topics. Mention your work projects and accomplishments.
7. If you worry about over-sharing, privately ask someone who was there if you were too much.
8. For sensitive topics (like outing yourself as LGBTQ), ask around the office. See if other people have brought those up before and what the response was then.
9. Work with a coach on strategies to get you comfortable with sharing more or sharing less.

10. Talk to a therapist on why you might not be comfortable sharing.
11. Ask someone you trust for their opinion on sharing personal information.

See Also:
Challenge 2: Setting Boundaries
Challenge 10: Building Relationships with Colleagues
Challenge 11: Social Media at Work

Take Action: Write down two topics you're okay talking about and two topics you're not okay sharing.

Challenge 66: Gossipy Colleagues

Private conversations are vital to everyday personal and professional life. Especially in companies, gossip can be a way to learn about what's going on and get ahead of other people. However, often gossip is used to spread negative information that is irrelevant to the company and serves only to bring people down. It is these negative types you should do your best to avoid.

1. Ask yourself if gossiping aligns with your values and goals. For some it is inexcusable. For others it's the only way forward.
2. Learn to differentiate between gossipers who share valuable work information and gossipers who just bring down others.
3. If you don't want gossip, keep away from gossipers so you don't get entangled in their mess.
4. Before you discuss any personal matters, make sure there are no eavesdroppers and that you trust who you're talking to.
5. Come up with set responses to gossipers. Something like "I don't appreciate talking about people behind their backs."
6. Keep your social media accounts private so gossipers can't stalk your pages.
7. If gossiping impedes your ability to work, talk to your boss or Human Resources about how to manage it.
8. Keep personal sharing to small talk so gossipers don't have information to use against you.
9. Find a colleague who keeps out of gossip and ask them how they do it.
10. Work with a coach to develop strategies for dealing with gossip.

11. If the gossip is having serious negative effects on your emotional health, talk about it with someone you trust, such as a close friend or therapist.

12. If gossip is a pervasive problem at your company, consider that this company is not right for you.

See Also:

Challenge 13: How to Have Difficult Conversations

Challenge 65: How Much Personal Information Do I Share with Colleagues?

Challenge 93: Company Culture Is Not Supportive

Take Action: Be a positive force in your team, sharing appreciation and joy towards your colleagues.

Challenge 67: Colleague Pesters You for a Date or Harasses You

Pestering and harassment can come in various ways. A colleague who doesn't know when to stop asking. A coworker who says inappropriate comments. Worst, someone who touches you without permission. It is one of the most frightening and upsetting experiences many people unfortunately go through at work. In some cases, you may not even have support within your company. Ultimately, you need to reach out and get help to deal with this problem.

1. Tell them clearly, "No, I am not interested. Please stop asking." Leave no room for doubt or misunderstanding.
2. Avoid interactions with this person when possible.
3. If you need to contact this person, either approach them with a trusted colleague or ask someone else to contact them for you.
4. Speak to someone who's been in a similar situation. It's important to let someone else know what you are going through, even if it's outside of work.
5. Bring up these actions to your boss. They may be able to intervene on your behalf.
6. Know your company's policies around harassment. If the person is stepping outside of what's allowed, you can mention this to your boss or Human Resources.
7. Know that in the U.S., repeated unwanted sexual comments, propositions, or touching can be considered sexual harassment and against the law.
8. If you are in the U.S. or employed by a U.S.-based company, you have the right to contact the Equal Employment Opportunity Commission if you feel you are being discriminated against because of your gender,

including repeated, unwanted sexual comments or propositions.

9. Reach out to organizations that can provide information and resources, such as the Rape, Abuse & Incest National Network (rainn.org)
10. Ask for an internal transfer to another team or ask your boss to not be paired with this person on assignments.
11. Determine if this kind of behavior is common in your company. If so, you may want to consider looking for work elsewhere.

See Also:
Challenge 2: Setting Boundaries
Challenge 13: How to Have Difficult Conversations
Challenge 16: How to Ask for Help
Challenge 84: Don't Feel Supported by Boss
Challenge 94: Company is Indifferent to Bigotry

Take Action: Identify one colleague, senior person, or Human Resource contact to reach out to about the issue.

Challenge 68: Colleagues are Bigoted or Hostile

Being discriminated against simply because of who you are is a terrible experience that nobody should have to go through. Unfortunately, many people are stuck in situations where their colleagues are bigoted or hostile towards them. Here are some ways to deal with them.

1. Let the person know it's not okay. Say something like "Please don't use that word." Hopefully, they will respect your wishes.
2. Bring the conversation back to the main topic. If you are at a meeting, you can say "Let's bring it back to the agenda."
3. Know your personal boundaries. While you shouldn't have to deal with any bigotry, you may be willing to let certain behaviors slide while others are a definite no.
4. Document incidents right after they happen. Who did what, who else was there, what exactly happened. Use this information when describing the situation.
5. Be cordial with the offender by helping them with work (only if you are comfortable doing so). They may be less hostile to you if you show you're willing to help.
6. Approach them in private. A one-on-one conversation can help make your emotions and hurt more understood by the offender.
7. When describing what happened, first state an observation then impact. "When you said this word, I felt slighted." Don't make it personal.
8. Find people who can support you emotionally during this time, such as friends or family. Look for support outside the company, since the situation at work may be complicated.

9. Ask other people if they feel uncomfortable by the offender's actions.
10. Speak to your boss about your colleague's words or actions.
11. Work with a coach to find coping strategies while you determine a long-term solution to the problem.
12. Contact Human Resources or a lawyer if the discriminatory language does not stop.
13. Notice if this behavior is common at your company. It may be a sign that this company is not right for you.

See Also:
Challenge 13: How to Have Difficult Conversations
Challenge 16: How to Ask for Help
Challenge 70: Colleagues Don't Respect Boundaries/Requests
Challenge 84: Don't Feel Supported by Boss
Challenge 94: Company is Indifferent to Bigotry

Take Action: Discuss the incident with a trusted friend or colleague.

Challenge 69: Office Romance

We spend most of our waking hours in the office or interacting with people from our company. Thus, it's natural that your relationship with your coworkers can progress as you spend time with them. However, what about when you develop feelings for a colleague? The answer will vary depending on your career standing, your office culture, and the people on your team.

1. Always get consent first. Even if you just want to joke around or flirt, don't assume that the other person is okay with it.

2. Know your office culture. Some workplaces prefer to keep interactions strictly business related. In more laid-back offices, it may be okay to do some light flirting.

3. Know your company's policies. It may be against policy to have romantic affairs with coworkers. It also goes without saying, but company clients are usually also off limits.

4. Avoid conflicts of interest. For example, don't give extra credit or opportunities to someone because you are romantically attracted to them. Consider keeping distance from them in professional engagements. Your company should have both conflict of interest and harassment policies you can review.

5. If you develop a relationship, keep the sharing to a minimum. Even when the relationship involves two employees, most details should remain private.

6. Consider if an office romance could impede your career goals. In some environments, an office romance may be interpreted as you not taking your career seriously, regardless of that being true or not.

7. If you've had bad experiences with office romances in the past, avoid them unless something substantial has changed about your work situation or personality.

8. Be careful when going for public displays of affection. You don't want to make your coworkers or teammates feel uncomfortable.
9. Remember that people will want to gossip and be nosy about your relationship. Know what you and your partner are comfortable sharing. Don't yield on those boundaries.
10. Keep in mind that you may get a reputation for office dating if you have a relationship at work. You get only one chance for an office romance.

See Also:
Challenge 2: Setting Boundaries
Challenge 65: How Much Personal Information Do I Share with Colleagues?
Challenge 70: Colleagues Don't Respect Boundaries/Requests

Take Action: If this is something you're considering, have a discussion with your friends or trusted colleagues about whether an office romance can work for you.

Challenge 70: Colleagues Don't Respect Boundaries/Requests

Sometimes, even when we tell someone how we like to be treated or what behavior we are not okay with, they go ahead and do it anyways. This can be incredibly frustrating, especially when you have gone out of your way to tell them what you want. In the best scenario, they just need a little additional help understanding what the problem is. In the worst case, they are intentionally uncooperative. Regardless, don't be afraid to stand up for yourself.

1. Tell the colleague that you feel uncomfortable with their actions. Be clear about this.

2. If you've told them about your request before, ask them if they remember. "Hey, remember when I asked you to not do that around me?" Sometimes people need a gentle reminder.

3. Make sure they understand what your ask was. Ask them to explain it in their own words. People generally like to be helpful, but they need to know what it is they have to do.

4. Ask trusted coworkers if they could intervene on your behalf when the colleague crosses your boundary or request.

5. Avoid interacting with the colleague if your work allows for it.

6. Talk to your boss about your colleague's actions. They may be able to intervene on your behalf or put some distance between you.

7. If your boss or colleagues are of limited help, reach out to Human Resources about the issue.

8. Consider getting a transfer to another team within the company so you do not have to deal with this colleague anymore.

9. If this behavior is excusable or common in your company, this may be a sign that the company is not for you.
10. If they are harassing you, consider consulting a lawyer to know what your options are.
11. Work with a coach to develop a strategy on how to get through this issue.

See Also:
Challenge 16: How to Ask for Help
Challenge 24: You Think It's Time to Move On
Challenge 84: Don't Feel Supported by Boss

Take Action: Write down any past incidents. Be specific about what behavior went too far. Use this information when talking to the offender or other people.

Challenge 71: Asking for a Letter of Recommendation

When applying for a position, managers will often ask you for letters of recommendation. Requesting this letter can be a frustrating or nerve-wracking process. Remember though, that the application process is about showing your potential manager that you are trustworthy, and one of the best ways to prove you have the trust of someone else is via recommendation letter. With an open and communicative mind, getting a letter of recommendation can be a seamless process.

1. First, ask your current and past bosses. They understand the impact and value of your work better than you can.
2. Second, reach out to people you've worked with in the past. They can vouch for your cooperability and skills.
3. If you don't have any other options and are fresh out of school, you can ask your professors.
4. Be clear about what the letter is for. Is it for a new job? For introduction to a new client? The context is important when writing the letter. Share this context so the writer can suit the letter to your needs.
5. If the letter is for another job, let your boss know before asking for a letter. Give them a timeframe for when you'd like to be done.
6. Give the writer what they need to know. This includes your resume, points you want to focus on, and when the letter is due.
7. Sometimes, the writer they will ask you to write the first draft. Take this chance to focus on your strongest points.
8. Create a list of your valuable abilities and skills. Show this list to your letter writer so they can include relevant anecdotes and examples.

9. Have a conversation with the writer about the letter. Remember, this is a collaborative project.
10. Make sure the letter begins with how the person is related to you. If they're your boss, say so!
11. Ensure the letter ends with strong approval for your application.

See Also:
Challenge 3: Networking
Challenge 4: Setting Goals and Priorities
Challenge 13: How to Have Difficult Conversations
Challenge 17: How to Interview for a Job
Challenge 80: Boss is Difficult to Contact

Take Action: Create an ideal letter of recommendation that you would love someone to write about you. The letters you receive will be different, but this gives you a good idea of what matters to you and what you should work on.

Challenge 72: Want More Visibility

It is natural to want to be recognized for your contributions and accomplishments in work. Unfortunately, many teams and companies fail to give their employees the recognition they deserve. You can look for opportunities that garner more visibility or get the word out yourself.

1. Consider your career job goals. What kinds of visibility can help you achieve those goals?
2. Ask for boss to give you a shoutout during a meeting or presentation. A good boss should be proud of their employee's work and delighted to share.
3. Talk with colleagues about your work contribution. They might not even know about what awesome things you've done.
4. Look for high profile projects within your company. See what projects a lot of people are talking about or asking to join.
5. At the beginning of a project, discuss how the project will gain visibility. Many projects often don't have a plan for visibility or dissemination.
6. If your company allows, post your work on social media. Tailor your posts to your work. For example, you can make videos geared to a general audience or make in-depth technical blog posts.
7. Ask yourself if you believe your current work deserves visibility. It's easier to get the word out when you are proud of what you're doing.
8. Consider if your work is appreciated in this environment. It can be hard to get visibility if your team's values are different from your own.
9. If applicable, consider publishing your results in a trade magazine or newsletter.

10. Look at what colleagues do to gain visibility.
11. Talk with your company's Public Relations department about your desire for more visibility.
12. Speak with someone you trust about your visibility issues. A therapist or mentor who knows you personally could see a problem you can't.
13. Develop a plan with a coach to get the visibility you want and deserve.

See Also:
Challenge 5: Making Progress on Goals
Challenge 51: Difficulty Speaking in Public
Challenge 59: Colleague Takes Credit for Your Work
Challenge 93: Company Culture Is Not Supportive

Take Action: Find one thing you've done and get the word out about it as much as you can within this week.

Part 5. Boss Challenges

Challenge 73: Boss Doesn't Lead

A good boss is often a good leader; a North Star shining in the dark, directing your day-to-day work towards a greater purpose. However, instead of that, your boss will provide little to no leadership. In those cases, develop strategies for getting what guidance you need from your boss, or look elsewhere.

1. Prioritize work that does not require your boss. Examples include important errands or tasks you are already knowledgeable about.
2. Think of situations where you require leadership. This can be project planning or when making decisions. What guidance would help in those situations?
3. Ask your boss for more direct guidance. They may be willing to lead when specifically requested.
4. When asking for leadership from your boss or other senior, be clear about your ask. Don't ask them to lead the whole project; ask for directions on planning or for their opinion on a specific task.
5. Remember bosses often are not required to be a good leader. They could have gotten their position for other reasons.
6. If you need advice or knowledge, reach out to colleagues who are experienced with your problem.
7. Contact people who have previously worked for your boss. Ask them how they managed with the lack of specific direction or guidance.
8. Remember you are not obligated to lead in place of your boss. That's their job. Additionally, if you step up too much, it may cause tension with your boss over power dynamics.
9. If lacking leadership is a major problem, consider transferring to another team.

10. Work with a coach on how to find leadership or lead yourself.

See Also:
Challenge 7: When and How to Obtain a Mentor
Challenge 16: How to Ask for Help
Challenge 33: Hard to Finish Tasks
Challenge 85: Don't Have Resources to Complete Work
Challenge 93: Company Culture Is Not Supportive

Take Action: Reach out to someone you trust about your problems at work.

Challenge 74: Boss Takes Credit for Work

You toil away at your tasks for hours or days or weeks. Then, when the dust is settled and the project is done, your boss takes credit for all your work! While your work is valuable with or without credit, it is frustrating to not get the acknowledgement you deserve. Though in this situation, it is up to you to find ways to get that credit.

1. Keep track of your accomplishments. Even if you don't get your due credit, at least you'll know your value.
2. Before confronting your boss, consider how they might react. Some may see asking for credit as a sign of disrespect.
3. Ask your boss for your name to be included in the credits. In the best case, your boss simply forgot or is not used to including credits for their subordinates.
4. Determine if bosses getting all the credit is just a part of company protocol. It may be outside of your boss' control.
5. Talk to colleagues unfamiliar with the project about your contribution. Get credit for your work through your own word.
6. Discuss with your boss about what kinds of work deserve credit. You might value work that your boss does not.
7. Look for a new project where you can take more credit or get more responsibilities.
8. Speak to coworkers who get credit from your boss. Are they doing anything differently from you?
9. Consider if your boss or company only gives out credit at appropriate seniority levels. You may need to wait until you've worked for several years or reached a certain position before obtaining listed credit.

10. Talk to people outside your company about how credit works in your industry at your level. There may be industry etiquette you are unaware of.

11. Research if your field has specific guidelines for assigning credit. For example, in medicine, all individuals who contributed substantially to a scientific manuscript are expected to be credited as authors.

See also:
Challenge 13: How to Have Difficult Conversations
Challenge 72: Want More Visibility
Challenge 81: Boss Lies
Challenge 95: Company Culture Overemphasizes Seniority

Take Action: Determine if this is a discussion to have with your boss or if you should go around them.

Challenge 75: Boss Gives Preferential Treatment to Others

While the workplace should be a meritocracy, where the most capable and hard-working are rewarded, rarely is that ever the case. Even worse, sometimes people who are less experienced or proven than you receive higher salaries or assignments that you've been eyeing for months. These situations are incredibly unfair and frustrating. They are indicative of a boss or a system that has failed you. However, there are ways to work around your boss and get what you deserve.

1. Take a breath. This can be an incredibly frustrating experience, but pure anger will not get you the treatment you deserve.
2. Talk with people who receive better treatment from your boss. See if they behave differently or if there is a pattern between them (such as if the boss prefers only attractive women? That could be a different kind of problem!).
3. Ask your boss if you are doing something differently than expected or even wrong. There may be a hidden expectation you were unaware of and could easily address.
4. Look up the average salary for your industry and see if you are being underpaid. This can be a concrete sign of preferential treatment.
5. See if other people get the same treatment as you. Talk with them diplomatically about their experiences. They can back you up in a discussion with the boss or Human Resources.
6. Have a discussion with people who work well with your boss about how to best deal with them. This can be other seniors at your company or former employees of your boss.
7. Confront your boss about the treatment. Use specific situations, like "Can you help me understand how Israr

received the past 3 assignments? I was hoping to get an assignment and would like to understand how you make decisions."

8. Talk to Human Resources or a lawyer if boss is not being cooperative. They will let you know what the rules or laws are and your options.

9. Consider if preferential treatment is common at your company. If so, this company may not be for you.

10. Talk to a mentor or trusted friend outside of your company for assistance.

See Also:
Challenge 13: How to Have Difficult Conversations
Challenge 54: You Feel Like You're Not Heard
Challenge 64: Backstabbing

Take Action: If you think you might be on the short end of preferential treatment, examine the evidence before you come to conclusions.

Challenge 76: Boss Does Not Mentor

While bosses are primarily responsible for making sure you get your work done, great bosses also take some responsibility for your growth as an employee and in your career. However, many times bosses do not provide any mentorship and are there just to ensure the work gets done. You can work with your boss to ask for the kind of support that you would like. Additionally, there are many other resources to find and obtain mentorship elsewhere.

1. Ask your boss for feedback on your work. Consider asking at the end of a project or long task, since your boss will likely be thinking about your performance already.
2. Schedule a one-on-one with your boss. Use this time to get to know each other better and to ask for mentorship.
3. Be mindful of what your boss is already doing for you. They may be helping you in ways that are not directly mentorship. Show gratitude for that help when approaching them.
4. Remember that many bosses are not required to mentor you. In this case, no matter how much you ask, they won't have to budge.
5. See if your company provides a mentorship program. These typically involve pairing you up with someone more senior on your career track. Note they may not be available at smaller companies.
6. Learn from your colleagues. You likely work with someone on your team who is more experienced than you are. Take advantage of their proximity.
7. Ask a trusted colleague for help in getting mentorship.
8. Instead of obtaining a mentor, learn to self-evaluate. You can obtain the feedback you want by making observations on your own work and reflecting

9. Keep up with developments in your field. Subscribe to newsletters or social media accounts related to your industry. This kind of information is normally given to you by a boss or mentor.
10. Attend conferences for your work. There, you can both learn about new developments and meet possible mentors.
11. Look into obtaining advanced certification or attending educational programs.
12. Ask Human Resources if your company provides any training opportunities.
13. Work with a coach for help if you want mentorship on a specific problem.

See Also:
Challenge 6: How to Evaluate Yourself
Challenge 7: When and How to Obtain a Mentor
Challenge 14: Want Feedback
Challenge 84: Don't Feel Supported by Boss

Take Action: Determine what kind of mentorship you are seeking, such as career mentorship or for a specific job. This can help you when talking to your boss or going outside for help.

Challenge 77: Boss Bullies You

When you are being belittled simply for being who you are or for doing things that don't harm others, that's bullying. Bullying is commonly associated with the school playground, but what's worse is when people you should trust and respect are the bullies. Worst of these is your boss. Regardless of who is being a bully, you can stand up for your right to decency and respect.

1. Remember you are not responsible for getting bullied. This is on your boss and your company for letting it happen.
2. Write down everything that's happening. When, where, who was there, what did your boss do. Keep receipts for when you need to describe the event in the future.
3. Consider if the bullying involves gender, sexuality, race, or religion. Generally, these actions count as discrimination or harassment and are illegal.
4. Find colleagues who are willing to stand up for you. These can be people you see with negative reactions or seniors with strong moral codes.
5. Remember that you deserve better treatment. Get emotional support from friends and family or a therapist.
6. Consider pushing back against the bullying. Sometimes a little response can make bullies back off. Remember to not put yourself in danger.
7. Speak to Human Resources or Corporate Compliance about the bullying incidents and what options are available.
8. Reach out to someone who knows your boss well for advice.
9. Discuss the situation with a coach and create a gameplan for dealing with the situation.

10. If it seems like your boss will come under no penalties for their actions, consider that this company may not be for you.

See Also:
Challenge 2: Setting Boundaries
Challenge 16: How to Ask for Help
Challenge 67: Colleague Pesters You for a Date or Harasses You
Challenge 93: Company Culture Is Not Supportive

Take Action: Having to deal with a bullying environment can take a heavy emotional toll. Write down your support network so you know who you can reach out to.

Challenge 78: Boss Asks You to do Work Outside of Official Duties

In most companies, you are hired to perform a specific role or set of duties. However, sometimes your boss asks you to do more than you have the time or ability to perform. Even worse, your boss can ask you to compromise your or the company's wellbeing. In these situations, know that there are systems in place to keep your work aligned with your job.

1. Go over your job description (usually included in your initial contract or offer letter). Make sure your boss' ask is not included in the list of duties.

2. Know your company's policies regarding additional duties. This information will be useful when you discuss the situation with your boss or Human Resources.

3. If the ask is illegal, consider whistleblowing. You have the right to not comply and to alert the proper authorities.

4. See if other people work outside of their official duties. This can be a sign of a larger company problem or at least help you find allies.

5. Speak to colleagues about how your boss is treating you. See if you're being singled out.

6. Find a senior who has previously worked well with your boss. They may be able to offer advice on how to avoid this additional work.

7. Reach out to people who have previously worked under your boss. You can determine if this is a repeating pattern or find advice for dealing with your boss.

8. Consult a trusted friend from outside of your work.

9. Work with a coach for dealing with these additional duties.

10. If you notice that this kind of behavior is standard at your company, consider that this company may not be right for you.

See Also:
Challenge 2: Setting Boundaries
Challenge 13: How to Have Difficult Conversations
Challenge 42: Want to Improve Your Organization
Challenge 45: Managing Multiple Responsibilities
Challenge 46: Difficulty Saying No

Take Action: Write down what your personal boundaries are related to working outside your job duties; determine if those boundaries are being respected.

Challenge 79: Boss Insults You in Front of Others

While a boss is supposed to be supportive and helpful, sometimes they are not. Instead, they may be mean or hurtful, even in front of other people. This can be a terrible experience to go through. You are worthy of dignity and respect, but you need to respond to this situation carefully and escalate only when necessary.

1. Keep list of witnesses. Pay attention if anyone responds in shock or disgust. They may be an ally in future dealings.
2. Consider non-confrontational responses in the moment. Say "That's not okay," or "I don't appreciate that." Do not snap back or raise emotions. Those are unlikely to help and may make the situation worse.
3. Keep track of when these incidents happen and what your boss said. Use these receipts when you need to describe what happened in the future.
4. Let your boss know afterwards that their comments were harmful. Hopefully, they will be understanding and work to improve themselves.
5. Talk to a trusted colleague about the incident and ask what you should do next.
6. Find a senior who knows your boss well. They may know something about your boss that you don't.
7. Consider your boss is from a different culture; insults were acceptable in the past but are now looked down upon. They are still not okay, but sympathy can help to cope with their behavior.
8. Ask a trusted colleague to stand up for you next time it happens.
9. If your boss' conduct is overly sexual, inappropriate, severe, or continues for too long, contact Human Resources.

10. Consider if these kinds of comments are accepted within the company culture. If so, it may be a sign that this company is not right for you.

11. If you have trouble finding assistance at work, consider consulting a lawyer who can tell you your rights in this situation.

12. Work with a coach on how to handle this high-stress situation.

See Also:
Challenge 2: Setting Boundaries
Challenge 9: When and How to Obtain a Therapist
Challenge 16: How to Ask for Help
Challenge 93: Company Culture Is Not Supportive

Take Action: Determine your goal for this situation and create a plan for reaching it.

Challenge 80: Boss is Difficult to Contact

Your boss is supposed to be your direct point of contact in regard to what work you are supposed to do and how. Despite this, your boss can be hard to get a hold of or won't even give you a response. In this case, figure out how to work around your boss' bad habit. Also, don't be afraid to respectfully bring up this issue with colleagues.

1. During planning meetings, try to get work that does not require your boss' direct input to complete. Don't let your boss stop you from being productive.

2. If it's been a while and you haven't heard back from your boss, send them another email or message. It should be no big deal, as long as you are respectful and don't incessantly message them.

3. Leave a note on your boss' desk or with their secretary (if they have one) requesting what you need.

4. Know your boss' expectations. Sometimes they expect you to just figure out what to do without having to tell you anything.

5. Contact somebody who works with your boss often. Ask them to relay the message for you.

6. Schedule a regular meeting with your boss where you can exchange important information with each other.

7. Flag your boss down before or after meetings. It's a lot harder for your boss to avoid you if you're already in the same room.

8. If the lack of contact severely hinders your work. reach out to another boss or your boss' boss. Let them know that your boss is the problem. Be sure to have concrete examples with the negative impacts on the company in mind.

9.   Talk to other coworkers about your boss' behavior and lack of contact. See if your boss is playing favorites or if they're generally like this.
10.   Discuss with your mentor how they deal with such a boss.
11.   If you find your boss' behavior not improving over time, consider that this team or company is not right for you.

See Also:
Challenge 10: Building Relationships with Colleagues
Challenge 15: When and How to Have Face-to-Face Conversations
Challenge 16: How to Ask for Help

Take Action: If you're waiting on a response from your boss, work on tasks that don't require them.

Challenge 81: Boss Lies

It's important to know the truth in your job so you can accurately perform what is expected of you and achieve your desired impact. But this can be hard if your boss often lies. This can range from little white lies or bigger lies that actively harm your work. Regardless of the lie, you need to develop a strategy for dealing with your boss' brand of mistruth.

1. Keep a record of your boss' lies. When someone asks for examples, have the record to back you up.
2. Reach out to people who were there. See if they heard and saw the same thing you did. Potentially ask for their assistance in making a bigger case.
3. Take notes during meetings on what your boss has said. If you think they're lying, ask your boss if you took the right notes.
4. You might be able to figure out why your boss is lying. For example, if your boss is afraid of looking bad, they may inflate projections or shrink timelines.
5. Remember you are not responsible for your boss' actions. Do your work diligently, and what happens to your boss happens.
6. Find someone trustworthy outside of your team. Verify your boss' claims with this person if you're unsure of the truth.
7. Speak with people who have worked with your boss before. How did they do it?
8. Meet with a coworker or senior who works well with your boss. How strategies do they have for dealing with the lies?
9. Read *The Asshole Survival Guide: How to Deal with People who Treat you Like Dirt* by Robert I. Sutton (See the For Further Reading section)

10. If are sure your company does not care about your boss' lies, consider looking to work someplace else.

11. Develop a plan with a coach on how to deal with your boss' lies.

See Also:
Challenge 13: How to Have Difficult Conversations
Challenge 42: Want to Improve Your Organization
Challenge 84: Don't Feel Supported by Boss

Take Action: Consider if lying is a common aspect of the industry you are in. If so, this may not be the career or field for you.

Challenge 82: Boss Has Temper Tantrums

While bosses should be mature, sometimes they can reach a supervisory position without being able to safely regulate their own emotions. While you should not be responsible for your boss' temper tantrums, there are ways to deal with these situations effectively. Mainly, make sure the people in the room are safe and prevent the situation from spiraling out of control.

1. Consider calmly saying "I'm happy to discuss this with you later" or "Please stop yelling." People are less likely to continue being angry if they see another person being calm.
2. If your boss is not a threat, wait for the tantrum to pass.
3. Don't escalate the situation by raising your voice or getting physical.
4. Make sure junior staff are safe. They should be protected first.
5. If your boss becomes dangerous, leave the room. You should not have to put your safety at risk.
6. Document incidents. Take note of when they happened, who was a witness, and how often they occur. Use this when building your case.
7. See if there's a pattern in the temper tantrums. They may flare up after talking to a particular person or in a specific situation. Look out for these warning signs and leave before your boss gets out of hand.
8. Consider that this behavior may have been acceptable for bosses in the past but is no longer. Regardless, your boss should be more mature, but having sympathy can help in dealing with them.
9. Contact Human Resources after an incident. You shouldn't have to deal with a dangerous boss.

10. Talk to a senior colleague who gets along with your boss. Ask them what they do in these situations.
11. Work with a coach to develop strategies for these situations.

See Also:
Challenge 2: Setting Boundaries
Challenge 24: You Think It's Time to Move On
Challenge 95: Company Culture Overemphasizes Seniority

Take Action: Take a moment and play back the last temper tantrum. What could you have done differently?

Challenge 83: Boss Has a Short Attention Span

Sometimes your boss will have trouble juggling multiple ideas or keeping track of complex ideas. A short attention span can be especially frustrating with your boss since they are your primary point of contact with stakeholders and the rest of the company. Though, it is ultimately a personality trait, and there are ways to adjust your behavior to accommodate for a boss like this.

1. Use quick and concise communications. Keep information to a few sentences containing only vital information.

2. If you need something from your boss, send out regular reminders to them. Don't flood their inbox; send once a day or every few days. Your boss may even appreciate the reminder.

3. During meetings, keep the discussion on topic if your boss tends to derail the conversation. Having an agenda can be useful for keeping track of what's important.

4. Ask your boss what the best way to communicate with them is.

5. Consider if you can grab your boss' attention with a key phrase like money or cost savings or fancy features.

6. For longer topics, don't talk to your boss immediately. First, speak with someone else first, then give a distilled version of just the main points to your boss

7. Give information to people who work often with your boss. This increases the amount of people who will tell your boss what they need to know, making it more likely that it will reach them.

8. Adjust your expectations of your boss. You may be used to working with a more attentive boss, and this new boss will take some adjustments.

9. Talk to someone who knows your boss well for advice.
10. Observe how other people work with your boss. See if they have any specific strategies.
11. Ask a mentor if they have any similar experience and what they did in that situation.

See Also:
Challenge 8: When and How to Obtain a Coach
Challenge 73: Boss Doesn't Lead
Challenge 90: New Boss

Take Action: Pay attention during your next meeting with your boss for any moments where they are especially attentive. Can you keep their attention for longer somehow?

Challenge 84: Don't Feel Supported by Boss

Your boss is supposed to be your biggest advocate, guiding you on your journey in this position and beyond. Often though, they fall short of that ideal. If you feel insufficiently supported by your boss, you can work with your boss to get that support or look for alternative means.

1. Read books or blogs about mentoring. This can give you a good framework for what you should expect from your boss or a mentor. See the "For further reading" section.
2. Think about what kind of support you want. Having a clear picture can help you when asking for support.
3. Consider what your boss has done for you already. They may have given you support in their own way. If so, don't neglect this support when you ask for more.
4. Outline your short- and long-term goals. Keep these in mind when determining what kind of support you want.
5. Take note of specific situations where you feel unsupported, like during a meeting or working on a project.
6. If you need help with work tasks, ask your colleagues for assistance.
7. If you need advice on your career path, ask a mentor.
8. If you need help with emotional needs, get support from a good friend or a therapist.
9. Determine your boss' position in the company and what resources they have. They may be unable to give you the support you want due to lack of time or experience.
10. See if there's anyone in your life who gets support from their boss. Ask them how they got it.

11. Ensure you have a support network outside of your work team. Remember you are more than just your value to a company.

12. Consider that the expectations for a boss might have changed since your boss was in your position. They might have not had support from their own boss. This is not an excuse, but it can help you understand where they come from.

13. While your boss is supposed to support you, ultimately it is up to you to find the support you need at work.

See Also:
Challenge 7: When and How to Obtain a Mentor
Challenge 10: Building Relationships with Colleagues
Challenge 16: How to Ask for Help
Challenge 93: Company Culture Is Not Supportive

Take Action: See if there's anything your boss needs help with. If you help them out, they may be more likely to help you.

Challenge 85: Don't Have Resources to Complete Work

Being in charge or a project or task can be stressful enough. It's even more stressful when you are expected to complete your project without the necessary resources. You need to find a way to either get what you need or work around those deficiencies.

1. If the resource is knowledge or expertise, get the appropriate training or certification. Usually, your company will reimburse you for attending educational programs related to the job.

2. Make a detailed project plan. What do you need, how much time do you have, and how will the work get done? Compare the resources you have available against what your plan requires to see what resources you need.

3. Look into how predecessors to your position made it work. It is likely that they had to work under similar circumstances to your own.

4. Ask for help from coworkers. They might know tricks to work more efficiently.

5. Send emails to potential suppliers to get the resources that you need.

6. Prioritize asking for intangible resources, like more time or knowledge. Hard resources, like money or physical supplies, can be hard to get from project stakeholders.

7. Consider collaborating or bargaining with another group. What do they have that you need and vice versa? Perhaps you have extra staff time and they have extra knowledge.

8. Over the long term, do not be satisfied with being under-resourced. Make it clear to your superiors that you are working with less than you need. Otherwise, you will be given the expectation of being a miracle worker.

9.   Look into what resources other teams have available for similar projects. If they have more than you, bring that discrepancy up to your boss.

10. if you are continually under-resourced, consider that this company does not treat you right and it is time to look elsewhere.

11. Work with a coach to navigate this tricky situation.

See Also:
Challenge 16: How to Ask for Help
Challenge 42: Want to Improve Your Organization
Challenge 58: Colleague Doesn't Contribute
Challenge 84: Don't Feel Supported by Boss

Take Action: What resource is your most dire need? Come up with a plan to work around that missing resource or to get the more of it.

Challenge 86: Boss Has Unreasonable Expectations

Unreasonable work can take on many different forms. You can be asked to do too much in too little time. You can be given work that is far too difficult for your career or skill level. Your boss can be an endless perfectionist. Regardless, it is important that you feel capable of tackling and completing the work assigned to you.

1. Discuss with your boss about exactly what their expectations are. If they say something different later, you can refer back to this discussion.
2. Ask for help from a colleague. You may be surprised at how likely people are willing to help out. Note that this is a temporary solution, since your colleague likely has their own work to deal with.
3. Create a project workplan. This can be a simple list of tasks or a timeline of what needs to happen. With your workplan, identify tasks that can be outsourced to colleagues or external help. Go over your workplan with your boss. Identify which specific areas of the plan make your boss' expectations unreasonable.
4. Ask for training. This can give you knowledge or skills your boss may assume you already have.
5. Discuss and compare expectations with your coworkers. If you notice unequal expectations from your boss, you can bring this up in a discussion with management or HR.
6. Consider that your boss may be trying to challenge you. If the challenge is reasonable, it can be an opportunity to grow in your skills or career.
7. Consider that expectations which were once doable for you are now unreasonable. It's okay to work differently as your priorities and responsibilities change over time.

8. Consider that your boss may not be used to working with people at your age. They can be used to working with older people or who grew up before you did.

9. Consider that high expectations may be normal in this company, even outside of your boss. Ask yourself it this is the environment that you want to work in

10. Discuss with someone you trust (mentor, colleague, friend) about your boss' expectations. They can confirm your hunch or inform you of the norms for your job or industry.

11. Consider that this job or position may no longer be right for you

See Also:
Challenge 2: Setting Boundaries
Challenge 13: How to Have Difficult Conversations
Challenge 43: Too Many Projects/Tasks
Challenge 91: Company Culture is Overly Competitive

Take action: Identify one part of your boss' expectations you find unreasonable. Then, think of a way to make that work easier.

Challenge 87: Boss Makes Bad or Unethical Decision

Your boss is supposed to be someone you can trust to make the right call when the team needs it. However, not all bosses are perfect. Your boss can make a bad call, or at worst, a downright unethical decision. This can be incredibly disappointing coming from someone you should trust. In this case, there are steps you can take to make the situation a bit better and to help you process the incident.

1. Ask yourself why you think it's a bad decision. Is it a cultural or personal belief? Or do you have some understanding of the industry which informs the decision?

2. Have a diplomatic conversation with your boss about it. Be careful to respect your boss' authority. You may want to ask your boss if they can explain their reasoning so you can better understand their decision. Additionally, make sure you have a good explanation for why you disagree with your boss.

3. Determine if this decision affects your current work or your future prospects on the team. You don't want your boss' decision to affect your career prospects.

4. Learn what caused your boss to make this mistake. Was it a personal decision? Did they choose the best decision out of multiple bad options? They usually have a reason.

5. Talk to other coworkers about the decision. They can provide some perspective that you might be missing on the situation.

6. Ask your mentors or other senior staff for what they would've done.

7.   Notice if this is a trend. Sometimes people make one-off mistakes. Other times, it's a long-term pattern. This can inform your future plans for this team or job.

8.   However bad you think the decision is, don't get angry at your boss or with your work. Your emotions are valid, but not always helpful.

9.   Think about other times your boss made better decisions or was helpful. This does not excuse an unethical decision, but knowing your boss' good points can help you cope with their mistake.

10.   If you want to become a boss one day, keep this mistake in mind so you don't repeat it.

11.   If the decision was a grave offense, consider switching teams or looking for another company.

12.   Work with a coach to navigate this tricky professional situation.

13.   If the situation has triggered a strong emotional response from you, talk about it with close friends or a therapist first. Doing so can help you make the best decision going forward.

See Also:
Challenge 1: Determining Your Values
Challenge 13: How to Have Difficult Conversations
Challenge 26: How Do I Know if My Career or Work is Ethical?

Take Action: Write down what the situation was, what your boss decided to do, and why it was a bad decision. Articulating the issue can help you when discussing it with other people.

Challenge 88: Boss Undermines You

While your boss should be supportive of you and your work, some bosses are not. They belittle your work, cut your credit, and blame you for problems. Although incredibly frustrating, you need to work around this behavior.

1. Talk with your boss about how you would like to be treated.
2. Be clear with your boss about how their behavior makes you feel. Be careful to not come off as accusatory.
3. Ask your boss why they treat you like this. There may be good intentions misapplied.
4. Remember that behaving out of anger or frustration will not get the results you want. Those emotions are valid, but don't let them control you.
5. Don't undermine others in kind. Be respectful of others
6. Ask your colleagues if they have also been undermined by your boss. How do they deal with it?
7. Read *The Asshole Survival Guide: How to Deal with People who Treat you Like Dirt* by Robert I. Sutton (See the For Further Reading section).
8. Work with a coach on how to handle these situations.
9. Ask Human Resources for a transfer to a different team.
10. Check if this behavior is acceptable in your company. If so, this could be a sign to move on.

See Also:
Challenge 54: You Feel Like You're Not Heard
Challenge 74: Boss Takes Credit for Work
Challenge 75: Boss Gives Preferential Treatment to Others
Challenge 95: Company Culture Overemphasizes Seniority

Take Action: Think about what you are willing to work through to reach your goals.

Challenge 89: Boss Suggests It's Time to Move On

While we do our best in our work, sometimes we get called in by our boss and it becomes known that it's time for us to move on. Do not fret! Leave your current job with grace and plan for the future.

1. Ask if this means you are getting fired. There is a large difference between being forced to leave and suggesting that it's time to leave.

2. Ask your boss how much time you have left before you are forced to leave. Hopefully you will have at least a week. At worst, you'll have to leave immediately.

3. Ask – nondefensively -- what the reasoning is behind the decision. Tell your boss that you'd like to know what to improve on for your next job.

4. Update your resume with your latest experiences. Get it down on paper while it's fresh in your mind.

5. Ask if this decision is final. Sometimes your boss may be giving you a heads up about a decision that is coming down the line.

6. Talk with Human Resources about details such as keeping insurance, what'll happen to your 401k, and the possibility of a severance package.

7. Figure out what you must do before you leave. Are there any projects you need to finish or important information you need to share?

8. Make a list of next steps after you're finished with your current job. This can include applying to more positions or reaching out to old contacts.

9. Talk with colleagues you've worked with before you go. Get their contact info so you can stay in touch.

10. Remember that this is not the end of your career. There will be other opportunities for you in the future.
11. Work with a coach to develop a plan on how to navigate this change in your life.

See Also:
Challenge 4: Setting Goals and Priorities
Challenge 17: How to Interview for a Job
Challenge 18: Starting a New Job
Challenge 71: Asking for a Letter of Recommendation

Take Action: Write down one thing you learned at this position or would like to do differently for your next job.

Challenge 90: New Boss

Colleagues come and go. So too will your bosses. The period of transition to a new boss can be a stressful time, especially if your former boss was a strong leader. While it's ultimately up to your new boss, you can do your part to make the transition successful. It's just like any new relationship; you put in the effort to get to know each other and see how you work together. This advice can also be used for getting a new job or joining a new team.

1. Make yourself available to the boss. This can be an introductory email or slack message or a quick conversation in the office.
2. Be active in your first meetings with boss so they get to know you better.
3. Schedule a one-on-one meeting with your new boss to exchange information and expectations.
4. Tell your boss what your responsibilities and accomplishments have been up to this point. While they will treat you differently than your former boss, giving your new boss this context can help in their decision making.
5. If you're unsure about something, always ask. Open communication is key when transitioning to a new boss.
6. Discuss work expectations. Even if your job duties are the same, every boss has a different way they want things done.
7. Research your new boss. See what perspectives and experience they have to offer.
8. Don't say "but our old boss did it this other way." If your new boss' changes impact the productivity of the team, approach the issue from the perspective of increasing productivity instead.

9. Understand that no matter what, teams change. This change can be for better or for worse. It may also be better in some ways and worse in others.

10. Suggest people in company who would be helpful for your boss to know

See Also:
Challenge 10: Building Relationships with Colleagues
Challenge 15: When and How to Have Face-to-Face Conversations
Challenge 18: Starting a New Job
Challenge 73: Boss Doesn't Lead

Take Action: Set aside time to get to know your new boss.

Part 6. Company Challenges

Challenge 91: Company Culture is Overly Competitive

While a company is about people working together to achieve a common goal, some corporate environments feel like a medieval court, with colleagues constantly at each other's throats. This can be a frustrating and stressful environment to work in, especially if you yourself are not competitive. You can find a way to navigate this environment while keeping true to how you want to work.

1. Take note when over competitiveness leads to bad work outcomes. For example, sometimes people withhold useful information just to make someone look bad. If you collect a long list, show it to your boss.

2. Consider if competitiveness is required in your career. This is a good question to ask a mentor or online interest groups.

3. Don't compromise on your values. Being competitive shouldn't require you to act unethically.

4. Determine what the results of not being competitive would be. Will you be rated on competitiveness during your performance reviews? Or do they care more about how good your work is on its own merits?

5. Collaborate with people in a way that both sides benefit. Competitive people may be willing to collaborate when there is something in it for them.

6. Find individuals who do not like being competitive but do well regardless. What do they do differently that allows them to succeed?

7. Ask for help from your boss or people who depend on you for work. They will be more likely to help you since your productivity helps them.

8. Remember that changing the culture of an entire company is difficult. At best, you can foster a more collaborative culture among your team or peers.

9. If you find that the competitiveness regularly impedes your work or your health, consider that this company is a bad fit for you.

10. Ask a mentor how they deal with overly competitive environments.

11. If you find yourself stressed out about being competitive, talk to a therapist.

See Also:
Challenge 2: Setting Boundaries
Challenge 35: Feel Isolated
Challenge 37: Feel Negative about Work
Challenge 93: Company Culture Is Not Supportive

Take Action: Pay attention to situations where people seem to be more competitive than others. This can be around a certain high-level executive or around a certain skill set. Avoid these situations if possible.

Challenge 92: Not Sure Where to Go for Help

It can be frustrating to be met with a challenging problem but then find that your colleagues are unavailable or unhelpful. You end up confused with nowhere to go for help. Thankfully, there are many resources and techniques available to finding assistance outside of your team.

1. Turn your problem into a question and put it into Google. There's a good chance that someone else ran into a similar issue before.
2. Join an online community in your field. This can discussion forums, a community Discord server, or a Slack group. Public ones usually welcome people to ask questions and for advice.
3. If your problem is specific, try phrasing it in more general terms when asking for help. Common problems are likely to have more solutions available online.
4. Read books or articles related to your field. You may find a solution while looking at something completely different from your problem.
5. Don't blame yourself for not getting help. This is a failure of your team and company. Proper resources to find help and do your job should be made clear and accessible to you.
6. Try writing about the problem or talking it over with a friend. Articulating the issue with words can lead to inspiration.
7. Talk to someone who is good at giving help or pointing you in the right direction. This can be a kind coworker or a good friend.
8. Ask people for advice or get a group together for a brainstorming session.

9. Go to local professional clubs for help. There is likely a group or meetup centered around your field where you can network and ask questions.
10. Wait. Sometimes problems solve themselves without you having to do anything.
11. If you need specialized long-term help, consider obtaining a mentor, coach, or therapist.

See Also:
Challenge 7: When and How to Obtain a Mentor
Challenge 8: When and How to Obtain a Coach
Challenge 16: How to Ask for Help
Challenge 19: Understanding Hierarchy at Work
Challenge 93: Company Culture Is Not Supportive

Take Action: Think about how you can describe the problem in simplest terms. Break the problem down into its key parts and try to tackle them one at a time.

Challenge 93: Company Culture Is Not Supportive

If you find that your coworkers are unresponsive, your boss is nowhere to be found, or upper management and Human Resources are indifferent to what you need, you may be in the unfortunate situation of being in an unsupportive company culture. Recognize this problem, what you would like to be changed, and see if you can make that change.

1. Imagine what your ideal supportive company culture would be like. For example, would you be okay with having just a supportive team? Or would you like some formal acknowledgement from the company? Consider what is likely to be realistic at your level of seniority.

2. Consider if your company culture can even change on this front. Is management simply ignorant on the workers' needs? Or is it an ingrained value that employees should not need help?

3. Take small actions to help colleagues feel more supported. This includes complimenting people when they do a good job or offering help without asking. Make the company change start with you.

4. Find coworkers who are supportive regardless of the company culture. Build a small group of supportive employees and let others know that your group exists.

5. Bring up the idea of a mentorship or similar program to your boss or Human Resources.

6. Speak to friends or past colleagues to learn how their companies offer support. Consider proposing these solutions to a manager to implement at your own company.

7. Tell your boss that you are not getting enough help to finish your work. Have concrete examples of where some

assistance would've made a difference in the outcome of a project.

8. Remember that changing the culture of an entire company is a difficult task for any single individual. It can take a long time and might not even work out for you.

9. Work with a mentor to figure out how to find support either within or outside of your company.

10. Consider that this company will not be able to give you the support you need to thrive and that it might be time to look elsewhere.

11. Next time you are interviewing for a job, be sure to ask your interviewer if the company is supportive how you would like.

See Also:
Challenge 7: When and How to Obtain a Mentor
Challenge 8: When and How to Obtain a Coach
Challenge 9: When and How to Obtain a Therapist
Challenge 10: Building Relationships with Colleagues
Challenge 24: You Think It's Time to Move On

Take Action: Find support outside of your company. This can be friends, local professional groups, or online communities

Challenge 94: Company is Indifferent to Bigotry

While corporate culture has made much progress in terms of fair treatment towards all employees, many companies will still turn a blind eye to employees or even executives who are bigoted or mistreat those different from them. Don't be a passive observer; take note of what you see around you and find the appropriate channels to share this information.

1.   Write down incidents soon after they happen. Keep a list of incidents that occur, including what happened, who was involved, and why it occurred. Having the details readily available will help you sell your case to others.

2.   If the bigotry results in discriminatory actions against you or someone else, reach out to the victim and possibly a lawyer. Discrimination in the workplace is illegal in the U.S.; know what your options are.

3.   Consider becoming a whistleblower and speaking out publicly against your company (with the assistance of a lawyer). While a difficult ask, blowing the lid can lead to change for people who suffer under your company.

4.   Discuss what you see with trusted coworkers or people who have suffered from it. Compare notes about what you've seen.

5.   If you trust your boss, discuss with them the incidents you have encountered. While it may be outside of their control, having an ally with authority can be empowering.

6.   Be sure to keep safe. Poking around about incidents that can bring the company harm is generally frowned upon. Have a plan in case things go wrong for you.

7.   Research other companies that have been revealed to harbor bigotry. What happened to them? What about the

people that uncovered these issues? Think about how you would or should act in those situations.

8. Remember that you are not responsible for the actions of an entire company. You can do your part to call them out or even incite change, but it is not your fault that your company is like this.

9. See if there are any support or activist groups in your industry (such as "Women in STEM" or one for your own intersectionality). There, you can find assistance for your situation.

10. If the situation is too large or otherwise out of your control, consider how continuing to work here can take a toll on your health, career, and goals.

11. Have a discussion with a mentor about what to do in this situation. Your mentor might have seen or even experienced similar treatment in the past.

See Also:
Challenge 2: Setting Boundaries
Challenge 13: How to Have Difficult Conversations
Challenge 24: You Think It's Time to Move On

Take Action: Talk to someone about the issues you see, be it within your company or externally. Remember that you are not alone.

Challenge 95: Company Culture Overemphasizes Seniority

You're the best person for the task or in line for a promotion, but someone less qualified than you gets it instead, just because they've been around for longer! Terrible! While you may not be able to change their mind, you can make the case for why it should have been you.

1. Write down incidents where you think a senior employee was not the right person for the job. Consider if there are other aspects of the senior employee's performance that you might be missing. They may be more qualified than you think.

2. Determine if the senior person is really that bad. While they may get favoritism, there is a chance that they are actually good at their work.

3. Work with the seniority. Offer your help or ask for their thought process. They may notice your contributions and mention you next time a decision gets made.

4. Make sure your work gets noticed. If your results are good enough, you may be able to break the seniority wall.

5. Diplomatically discuss your perspectives with trusted coworkers. See if they agree with you.

6. If you trust your boss, discuss with them the incidents you have encountered.

7. Remember that even if you don't get your due credit or respect, you can still do a good job at work and work towards your other goals.

8. Acknowledge that not everything in life is fair. This is a problem with your company, not you.

9. If this continually happens at your company, consider looking to work someplace that better appreciates your contributions.

10. Work with a coach to tackle this problem.

See Also:
Challenge 72: Want More Visibility
Challenge 84: Don't Feel Supported by Boss
Challenge 93: Company Culture Is Not Supportive

Take Action: Talk to someone about the issues you see, be it someone inside or outside the company. Don't go quietly.

Challenge 96: Company Does Not Respect Gender Identity

Whether it's you or a coworker, your company should respect your gender identity and provide appropriate accommodations. In fact, certain actions can even be deemed discriminatory and illegal. Despite that, there can be subtle actions within the culture or the system of the company which do not respect people's gender identity. Here are some steps to take to make sure the issue is known and how to deal with it.

1. Write down instances where your gender identity is disrespected. Who was there, what happened, when did it happen?
2. Determine scope the scope of the problem. Is this a few people? Is it a cultural issue? Is it a systematic issue within the company (i.e., discriminatory bathrooms)?
3. Reach out to friends for emotional support. Dealing with this situation can be very taxing, so use your support systems.
4. Find an ally within the company. This can be someone who understands what you're going through or knows the severity of the problem.
5. Find other people who have issues with the way things are. Having a lot of people backing you can help make a case to HR or management.
6. If your company has a reporting system for such incidents, be sure to use it before resorting to other options.
7. Consult with a lawyer about what your options are.
8. Speak to Human Resources about what's going on. They may be unaware of what's going on within your company because it's not being reported.

9. Remember that discrimination against gender identity is illegal, and that the perpetrators can face legal action against them.
10. If the problem does not get solved or does not feel solvable, consider looking for somewhere else to work.
11. Talk to a therapist to help you process this tricky emotional situation.

See Also:
Challenge 2: Setting Boundaries
Challenge 16: How to Ask for Help
Challenge 24: You Think It's Time to Move On
Challenge 94: Company is Indifferent to Bigotry

Take Action: Speak to someone about what's going on.

Challenge 97: Company Performs Unethically

The hope for many people is that your work helps people more than it hurts. But so often, a company will take paths or make decisions of dubious standards and morals. What can you do if you find yourself in such a company? Take note of what happens and reach out to people.

1. Document unethical incidents. Keep track of what happened and who was involved. Keep this information on hand, especially if you consider taking actions in the future.

2. Determine if this decision affects your current work or your future prospects on the company. Don't let your current company's unethical actions affect your long-term career.

3. If especially egregious, consider becoming a whistleblower for your companies' actions. While unethical doesn't always mean illegal, you can find support by speaking the truth about what happens.

4. Think about what values could have led to unethical action. Usually, the people making the call think it's a good choice. You may be missing important context that makes the situation seem worse than it is.

5. Understand that every decision comes with tradeoffs. What is unethical may have been the better of two evils, even if that doesn't make the decision right.

6. Discuss what you see with trusted coworkers or close friends. Check with them to identify if there are other perspectives before concluding that what happened was actually unethical.

7. Be sure to keep safe. Being open about what's going on may put your job or even your career at risk.

8. Research other companies that have been revealed to have acted unethically. See what happened to that company and how the employees responded. You may find inspiration for your own case.

9. Remember that you are not responsible for the actions of an entire company. You can do your part to help and call them out, but it is not your fault.

10. If you feel like your company is indifferent or not willing to change, consider looking into working somewhere else.

11. Have a discussion with a mentor about what to do in this situation.

12. Reach out to a therapist or counselor for help processing your company's decision.

See Also:
Challenge 1: Determining Your Values
Challenge 22: Uncertainty Choosing a Career
Challenge 26: How Do I know if My Career or Work is Ethical?
Challenge 98: Company is Ignorant on Social Issues

Take Action: Talk to someone you trust about the issue. Practice articulating the event and why it was wrong.

Challenge 98: Company is Ignorant on Social Issues

No person (or company) is an island. No matter how big or small your company is, it has some part to play in the larger issues facing our society. Despite this, many companies are ignorant of or indifferent towards these issues. While you may not be able to change your entire company culture, you can take several steps to make these issues a more prominent part of your corporate life.

1. Get involved with social issues in your life outside of your work. Attend protests. Learn about what issues matter. Volunteer for charities and outreach groups.
2. Look for activist groups in your industry. Groups are usually built to target a specific demographic in a specific industry, such as women in STEM.
3. Actively support underprivileged peoples and minorities within your company. Even as a low-level employee, you can reach out to them, give them help when they need it, and make them feel like they belong.
4. Remember that if you belong to a marginalized group, simply being out and about within your company makes people similar to you feel more comfortable and like they belong.
5. Research how other companies in your industry handle social issues. Do they participate in events or have programs that can be implemented in your own company?
6. Find other people within your company who are engaged with social issues. Consider holding a meeting or creating a mailing list or group chat with those people.
7. Ask your boss or other seniors within the company if they are interested in growing the company's stance on social issues. Offer your knowledge of the issues. Having the support of leadership can result in fast progress.

8. If you notice systematic issues related to broader social issues within your company, bring up to your boss or Human Resources. They might not even be aware that those issues exist within the company.
9. Read stories and blog posts about how other people made their companies more engaged with broader social issues.
10. If your company feels indifferent and immovable towards social issues, consider prioritizing activism when looking for your next company.
11. Work with a coach to develop change within your company.

See Also:
Challenge 1: Determining Your Values
Challenge 10: Building Relationships with Colleagues
Challenge 11: Social Media at Work
Challenge 13: How to Have Difficult Conversations
Challenge 24: You Think It's Time to Move On

Take Action: Think about what marginalized groups interact with your company's work. Think about how you can reach out to give them the additional support they need.

Challenge 99: Company is Boring

Have you ever told someone where you work and be responded to with indifferent stares? Does your company feel like a gray, lifeless blob? Is your company just kinda boring? Well, you need to figure out what kind of work or projects excite you. Then, find a way to incorporate that into your company or find someplace that does.

1. Determine what your goals and priorities are. Does your company fulfill them? Is there something you can do to achieve your goals and priorities within the company?
2. Research what is new and exciting within your industry. See if what you found can be incorporated into your work.
3. Create a proposal for an exciting project that you'd like to work on. Show it to your boss or coworkers and see if they would be interested in carrying it out.
4. Determine what excites you. Is it working on new projects? Learning new things? Interacting with new people? Solving hard problems? Think of these when designing a course of action.
5. Spend time on interesting side projects when you're off the clock. This is helpful if you are unable to quit or change your current job.
6. Talk to friends about your company being boring and ask them for ideas. They may have some helpful advice or even be in a similar situation themselves.
7. Bring up the topic to trusted coworkers. They might feel the same way you do. Or, they might find something interesting about the company that you couldn't see alone.
8. Ask your boss if there any new projects going on inside your company and let them know you're interested in a change of pace.

9.   If you've exhausted all interesting opportunities within your company, consider that this company may no longer be for you.
10. Work with a coach about how to make your company more interesting.
11. Talk to a mentor about what to do with this finding.

See Also:
Challenge 5: Making Progress on Goals
Challenge 34: Unmotivated at Work
Challenge 47: Bored at Work

Take Action: Think about why you joined this company in the first place. Even if it wasn't exciting to you then, keep that reason in mind when you go in for work.

For Further Reading

Getting Things Done: The Art of Stress-Free Productivity by David Allen. (New York, Penguin Books, 2015).

Read Quiet: The Power of Introverts in a World that Can't Stop Talking by Susan Cain (See the For Further Reading section).

Influence: Science and Practice by Robert B. Cialdini. (Boston, Pearson, 2003).

Influence without Authority by Allan R. Cohen & David L. Bradford. (New York, John Wiley & Sons, 1991).

Triggers: Creating Behavior That Lasts—Becoming the Person You Want to Be by Marshall Goldsmith (New York, Crown, 2015)

The Asshole Survival Guide: How to Deal with People who Treat you Like Dirt by Robert I. Sutton. (New York, Houghton Mifflin Harcourt, 2017)

"How to Pick a Career (That Actually Fits You)" by Tim Urban (https://waitbutwhy.com/2018/04/picking-career. html, 2018)

Millennials' Guide to Work: What No One Ever Told You About How to Achieve Success and Respect by Jennifer Wisdom (New York, Winding Pathway Books, 2019)

Millennials' Guide to Workplace Politics: What No One Ever Told You About Power and Influence by Mira Brancu and Jennifer Wisdom (New York, Winding Pathway Books, 2021)

Millennials' Guide to Diversity, Equity & Inclusion: What No One Ever Told You About the Importance of Diversity, Equity, and

Inclusion by Lisa Jenkins and Jennifer Wisdom (New York, Winding Pathway Books, 2021)

Millennials' Guide to Management & Leadership: What No One Ever Told You About How to Excel as a Leader by Jennifer Wisdom (New York, Winding Pathway Books, 2020)

Acknowledgements

First, thanks to Dr. Jennifer Wisdom for approaching me in early 2021 in taking on this book. The work you've done for the Millennials'/Gen Z Guides series is inspiring and this book would not be possible without your original expertise. Thank you for believing that a kid like me could take on a project like this. Thank you to Cassandra Blake and Chelsea Matthews for helping to orchestrate the timeline and emails and all the other non-writing things I played little part in. Thank you to Emily Chauhan for listening to me whinge about the writing process for the latter half of 2021 and being an overall supportive friend. Thank you to Dan Dulguerov and my therapist Xinyu Sun for your generous support over the past several years. This book is only possible because of all of you.

Thank you to MINY Toastmasters for providing me a supportive community which has greatly expanded my professional abilities and potential. All my professional successes in the past couple years can be traced back to y'all. Special thanks to Felisha Howard-Lee, Suzanne Schwartzberg, and Beverly Howard.

Thanks to everyone who has been a positive force in my life over the past 2 years. In no particular order, thank you John Litag, Jordan Tantuico, April, Alcy Hart, Kate, Korin Lewis, Homu, the other homies at Consideration Cove, Max Del Rosario, Truffled Hut, Prism, Xander Remo, Katrina Remo, Leela Chauhan, Christopher Colon, Jona, Dusty Ashton, and everyone else I cannot remember currently.

Thank you Raefah, Serena, Rachel, and Claire.

Thanks to my parents for doing their best.

All of you make this worth it.

-Nora

About the Authors

Nora Del Rosario is a speaker and writer on Gen Z, relationships, and diversity. A programmer by day, she spends her spare time growing her speaking and writing. She has contributed to the Millennials' and Generation Z's Guide to Voting. Nora graduated from the Stevens Institute of Technology in 2021 with a Bachelor's degree in Computer Science and a minor in Literature. She is also a member of the National Speaker Association New York Chapter and the recipient of the Phil M. Jones Scholarship, a program to support promising young speakers. Nora is based in Jersey City, New Jersey, across the river from Manhattan. She can be reached on Instagram as @nora.betrue.

Jennifer Wisdom, PhD MPH ABPP, is a former academician who is now an author, consultant, and speaker, and principal of Wisdom Consulting. As a consultant, she helps curious, motivated, and mission-driven professionals to achieve their highest potential by identifying goals and then providing them with the roadmap and guidance to get there. Jennifer is the author of the Millennials' Guides series, including *Millennials' Guide to Work*; *Millennials' Guide to Management & Leadership*; *Millennials' Guide to Diversity, Equity, and Inclusion*; and *Millennials' Guide to Workplace Politics*. She is also the author of *Leaving Revolution: How We Are Learning to Let Go and Move On*. Jennifer has worked with complex health care, government, and educational environments for 25 years, including serving in the U.S. military, working with non-profit service delivery programs, and as faculty in higher education. She is an intrepid adventurer based in New York City and Portland, Oregon. She can be reached at www.leadwithwisdom.com.